Black & White Men

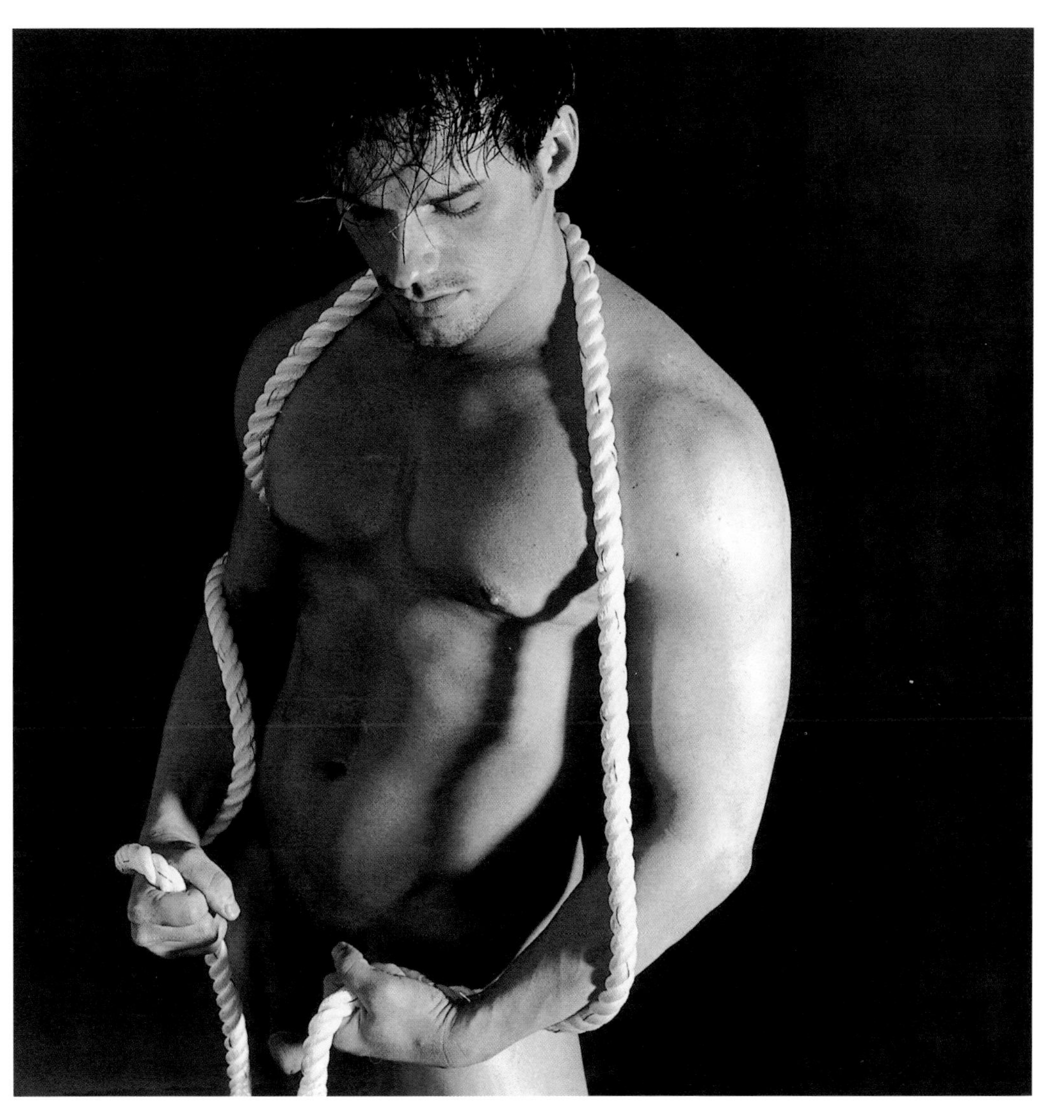

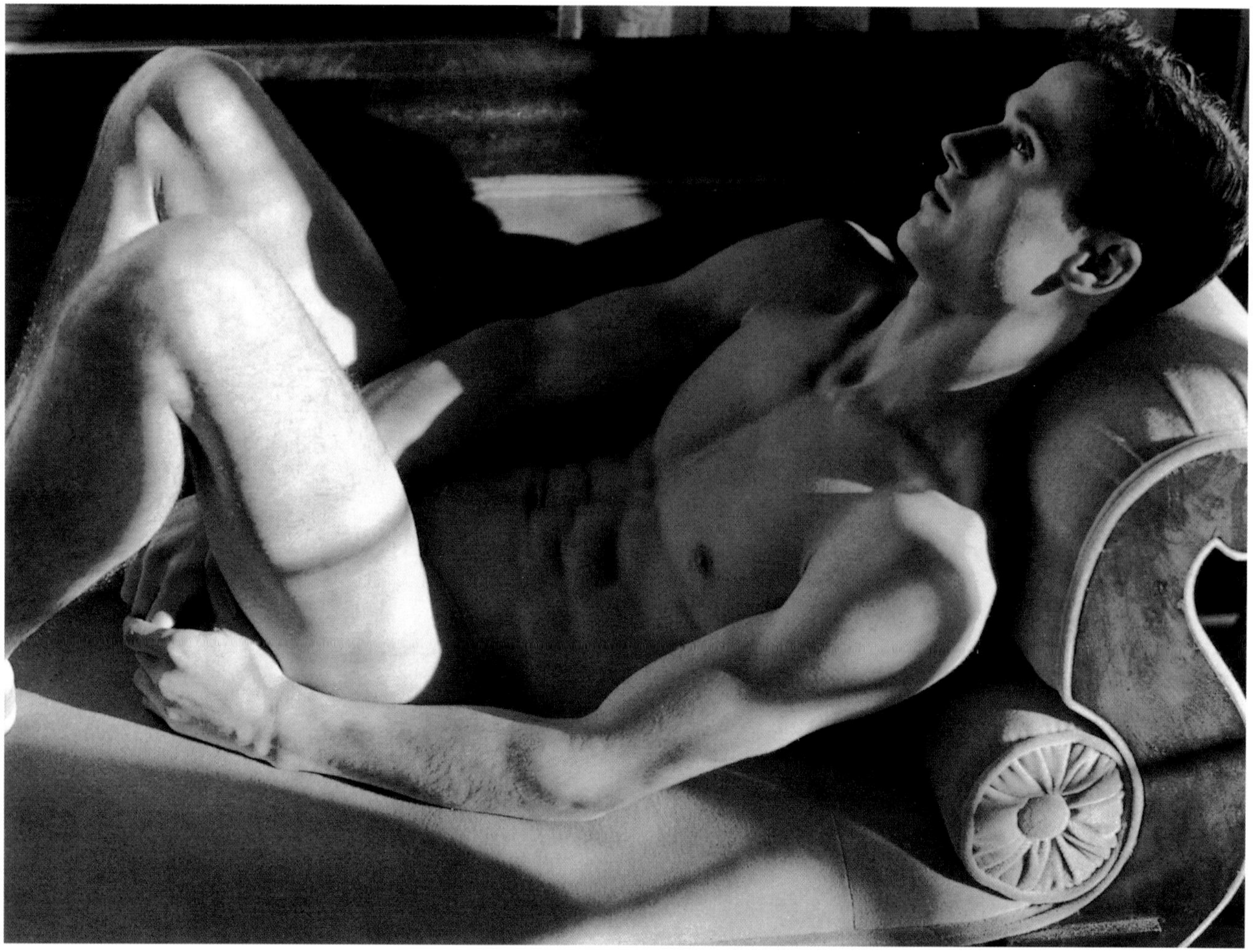

Black & White Men

Images by

James Spada

Foreword by

Nick Johnson

Pond Street Press

ISBN 0-9679908-2-3

Library of Congress Control Number: 00-134142

FRONTISPIECES:
Half title page: Damian in my studio, Brookline, MA, March 1998
Opposite title page: Michael on Laura Van Wormer's settee, Meriden, CT, December 1998
Opposite this page: Dante in my studio, Natick, MA, May 1999
Opposite foreword: Shane in Jonathan O'Leary's studio, Boston, December 1999
Opposite opening page: Thompson in my studio, Brookline, July 1998

First Edition / November 2000

Published by
Pond Street Press
P.O. Box 486
Natick MA 01760

Printed in Hong Kong

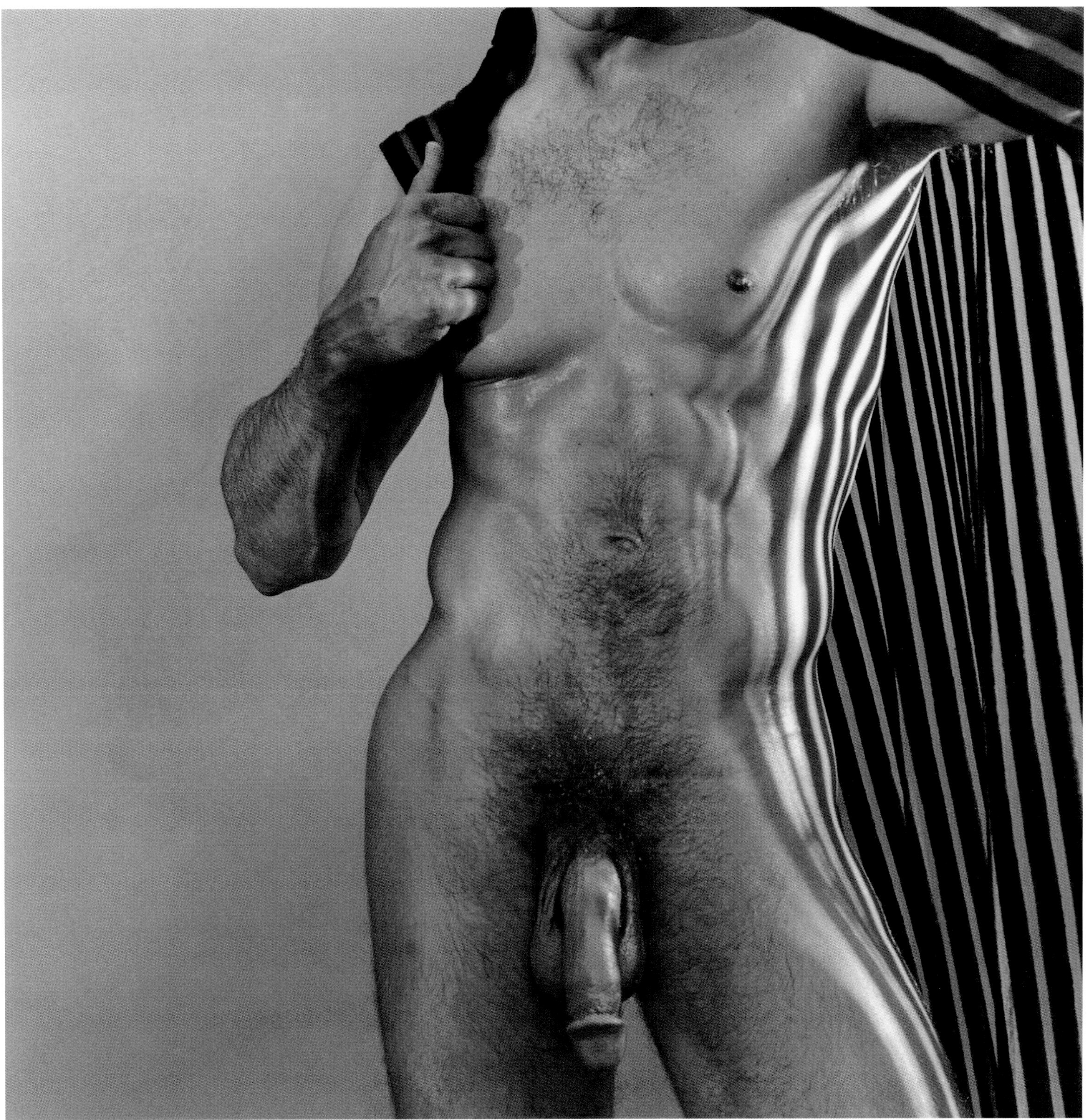

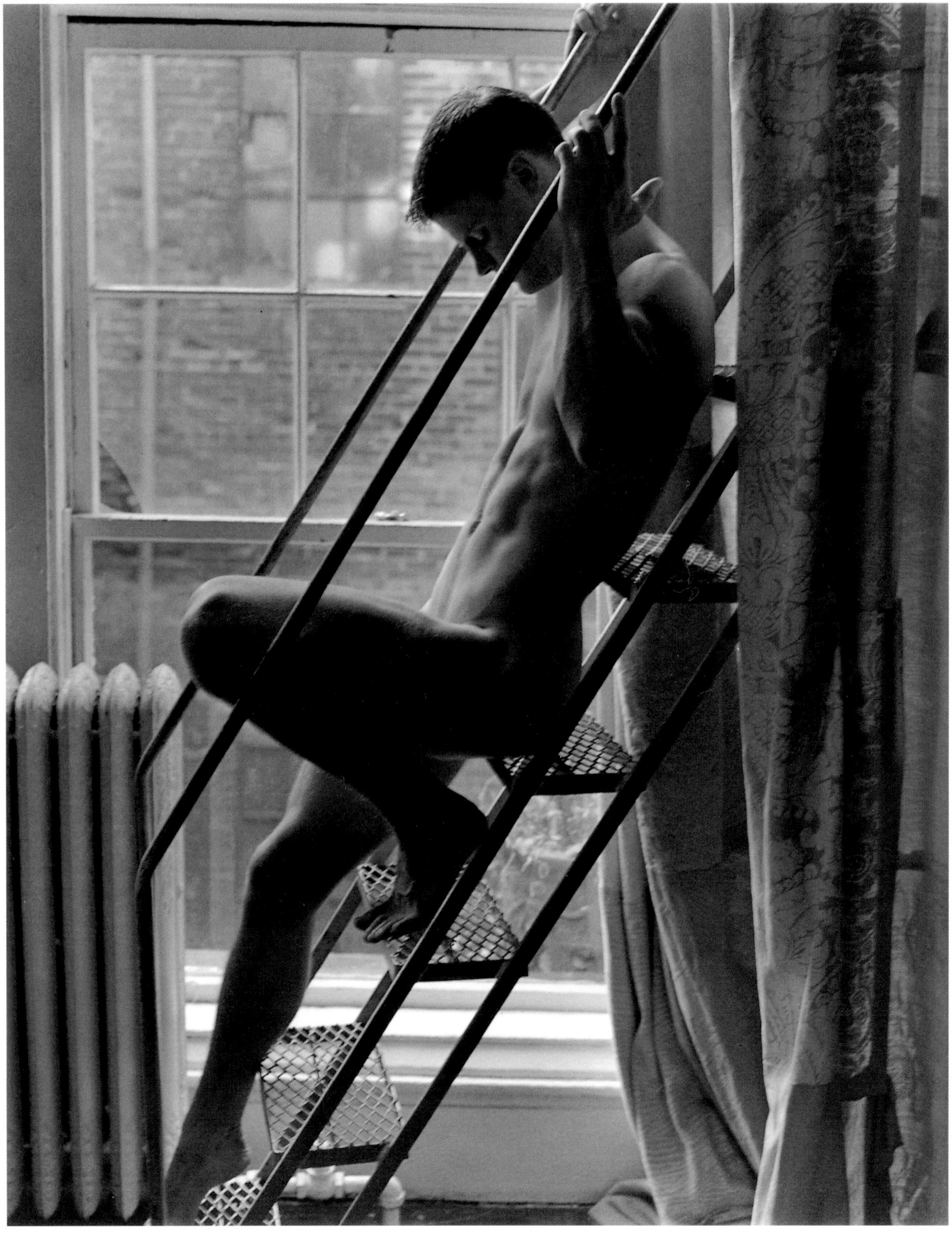

Foreword

BY NICK JOHNSON

James Spada is a gifted artist whose images are both beautiful and moving. Much of his work is reminiscent of classical painting and sculpture, particularly Michelangelo's statue of David. In these photographs one sees an idealized male form, muscles rippling, skin as smooth as marble, beautifully rendered through a masterful use of light and photographic technique.

While Spada's control of these formal qualities would alone set him apart from most photographers working with this subject matter, his images contain other elements that rarely find their way into male nudes and which give them their uniquely dimensional quality. The sensual eroticism that these photographs convey emerges not only from the innate grace of Spada's subjects but from the way he sees these men as an integral part of the light that describes them. Although often iconic, these depictions allow the models' personalities to surface as well, affording us an extra element of intimacy.

The beauty of the images in this book is more than skin deep, and complex in a way capable of evoking responses on several emotional levels. I hope the viewer will spend some time with them and look below the surface. It is sure to be a rewarding experience.

Nick Johnson is a photographer and instructor at the New England School of Photography in Boston. He also serves as the director of NESOP's Gallery One.

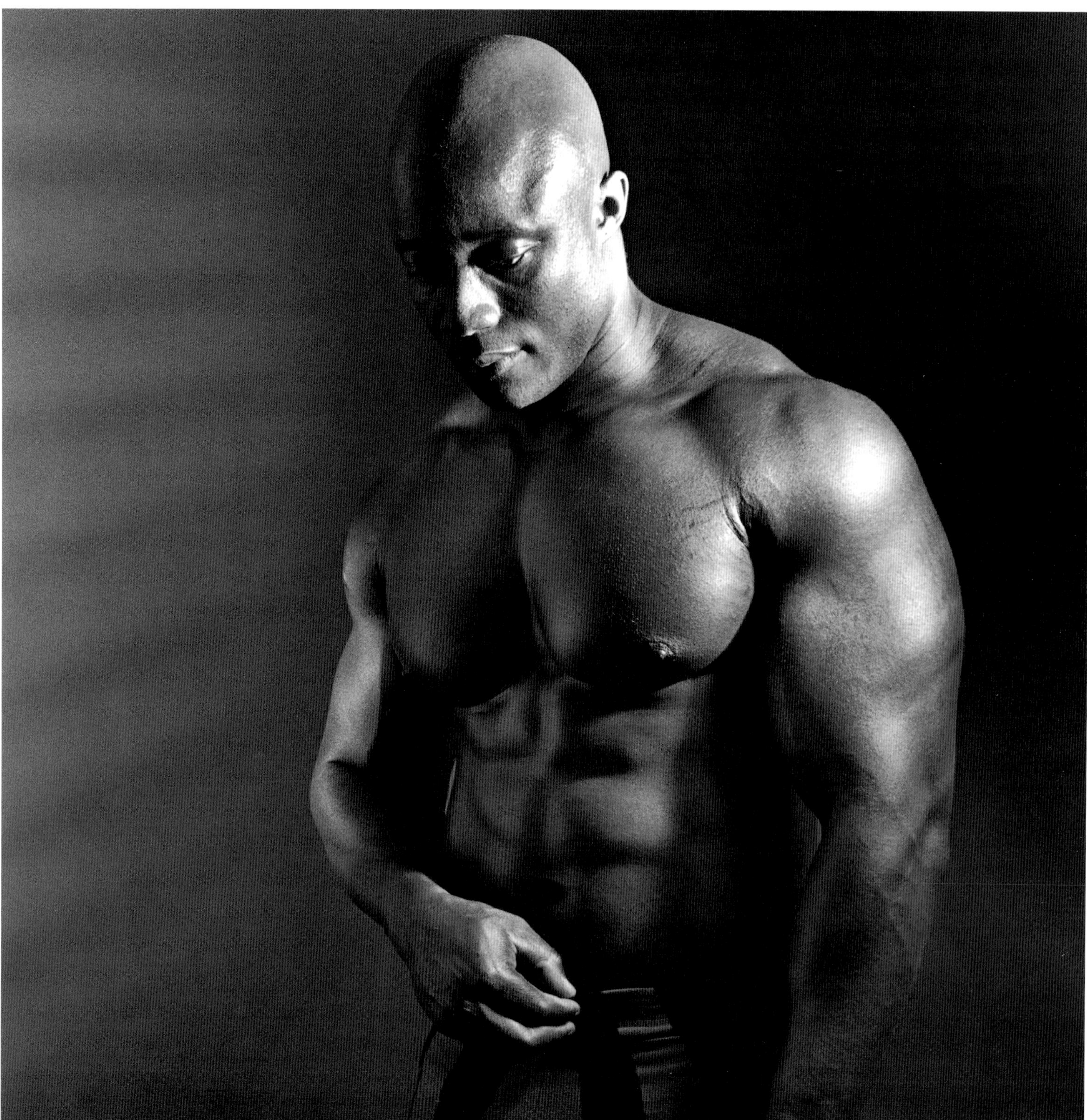

Black & White Men

Mike in my studio, Brookline, MA, July 1998

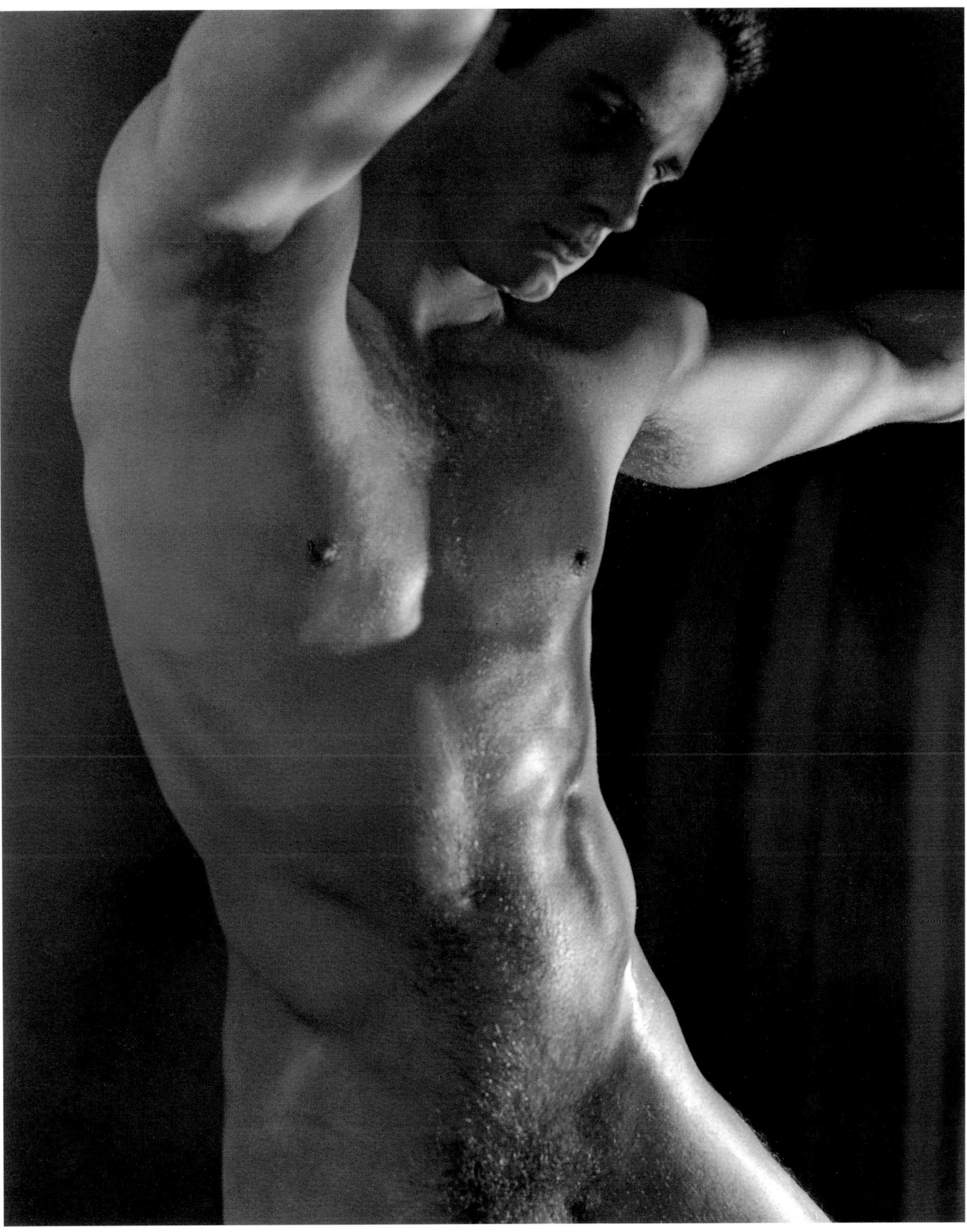

Mike in my studio, Brookline, April 1998

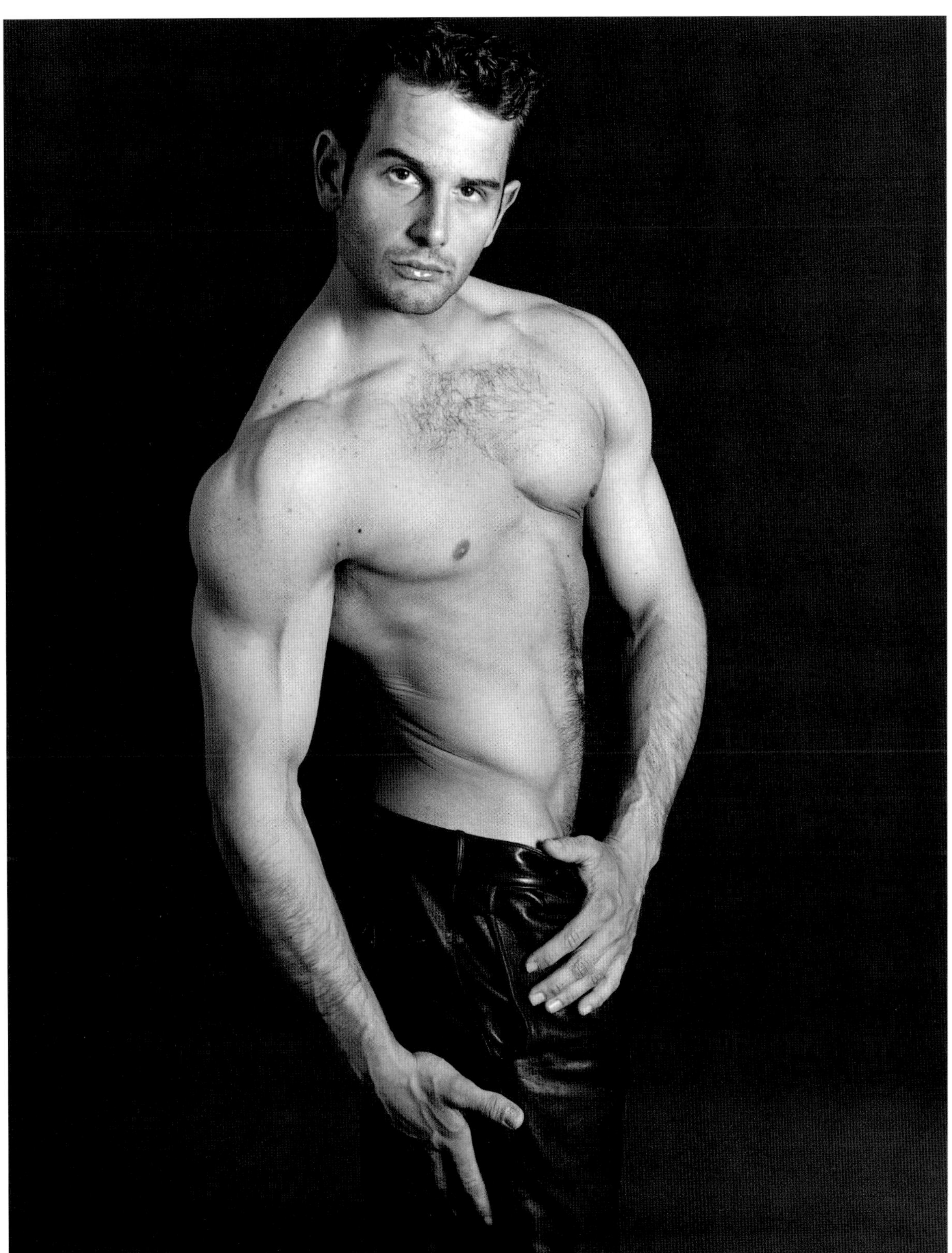

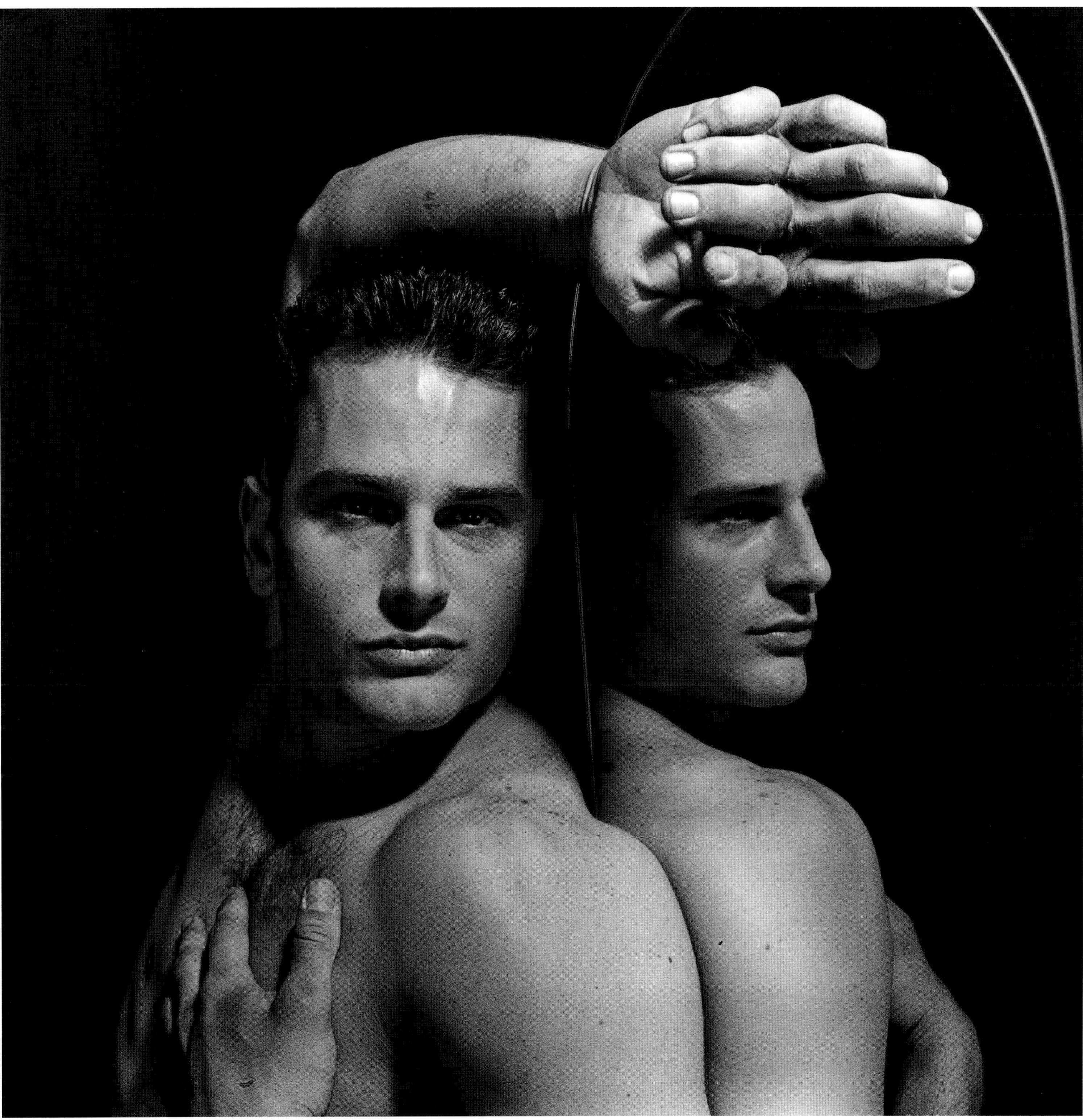

Mike in my basement, Brookline, April 1998

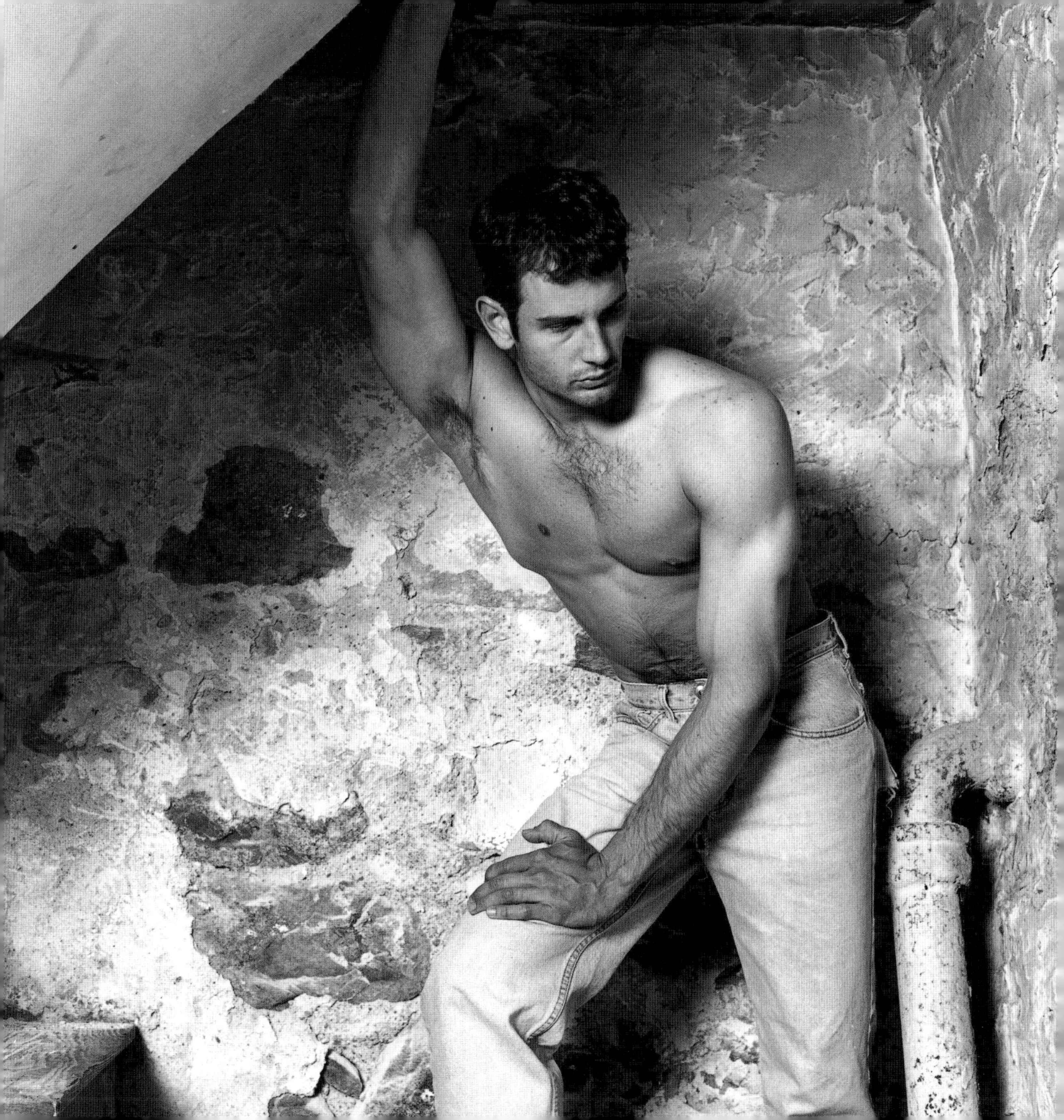

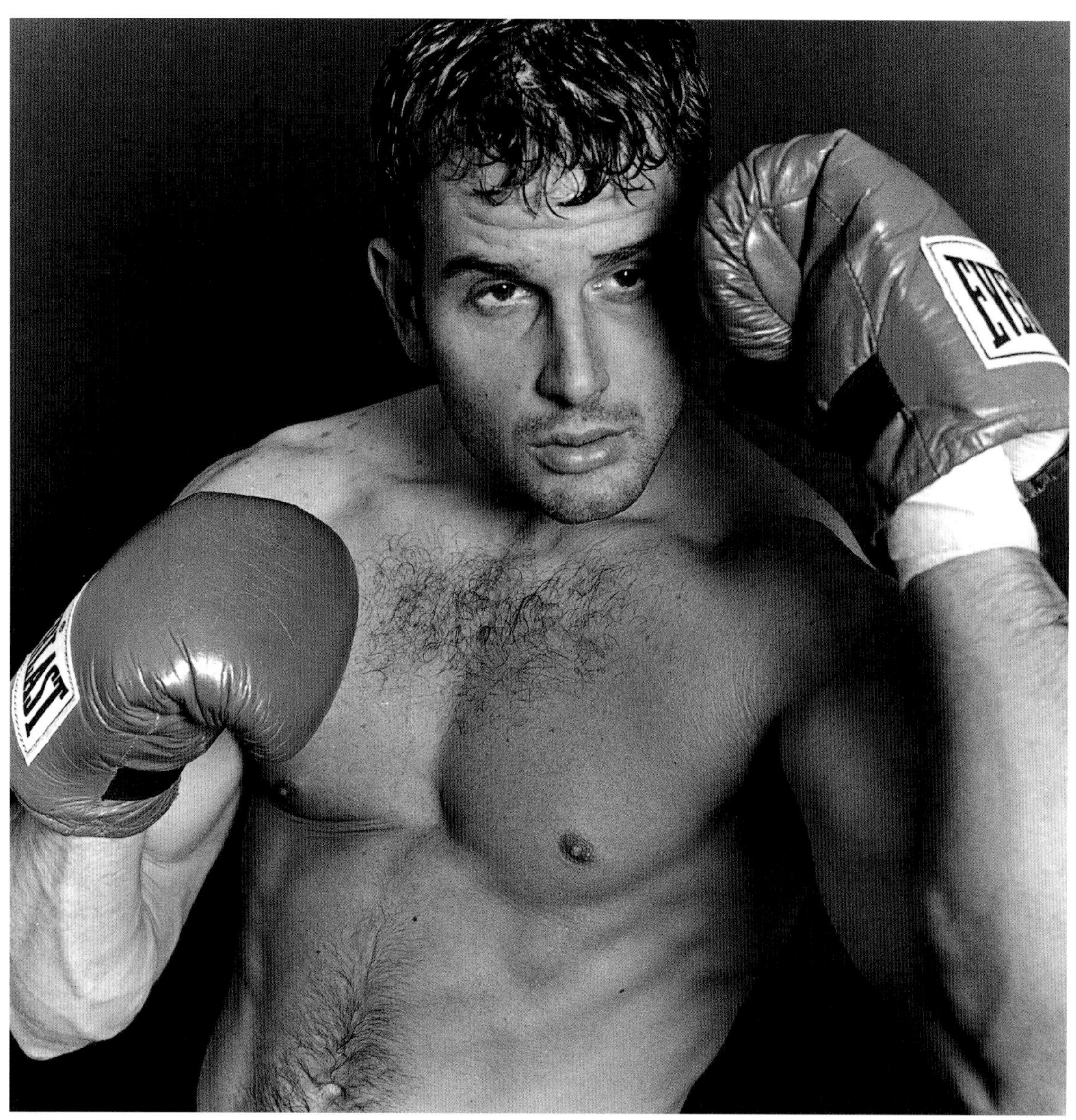

Mike in my studio, Brookline, April 1998

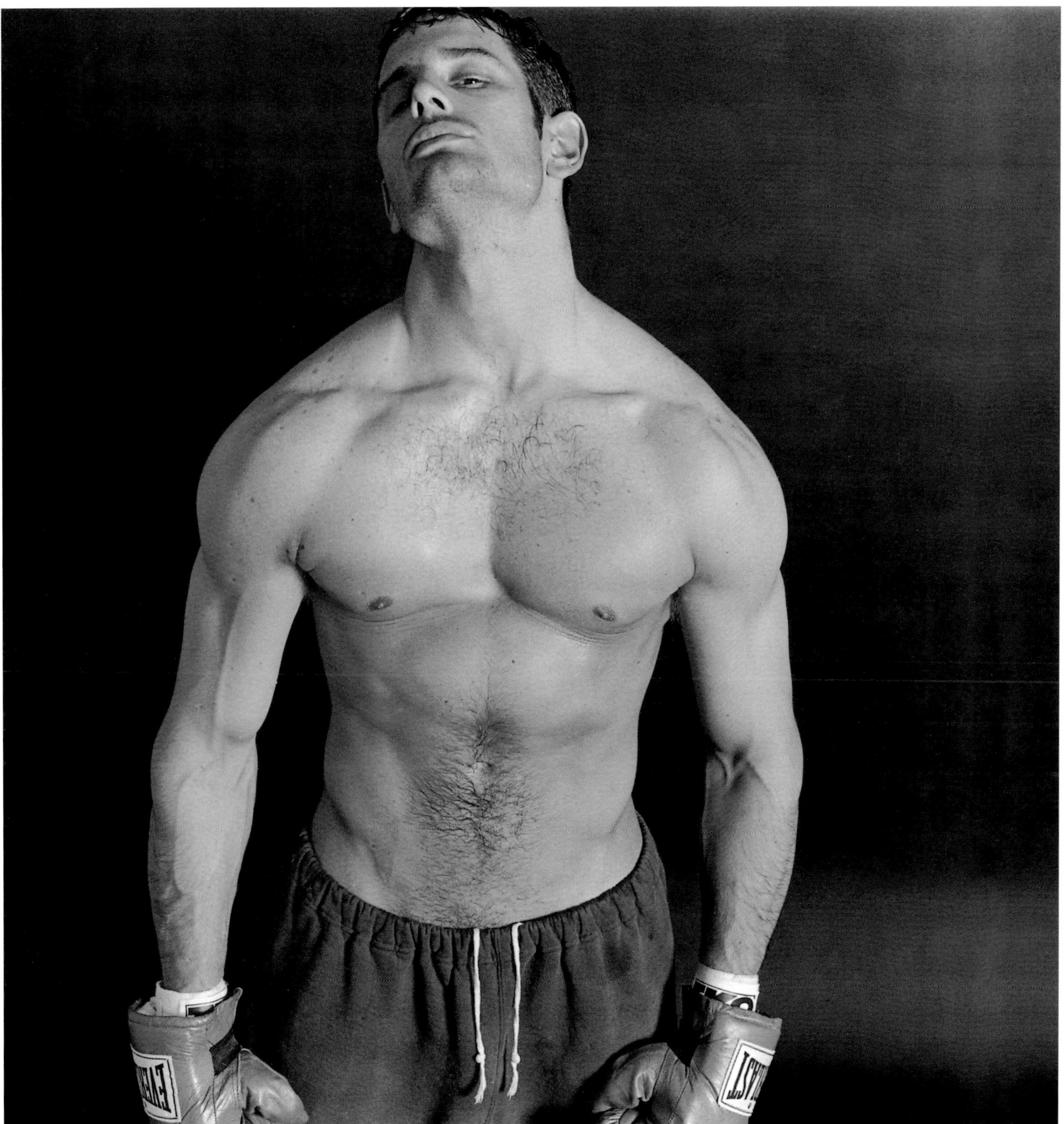

Thompson in my studio, Brookline, July 1998

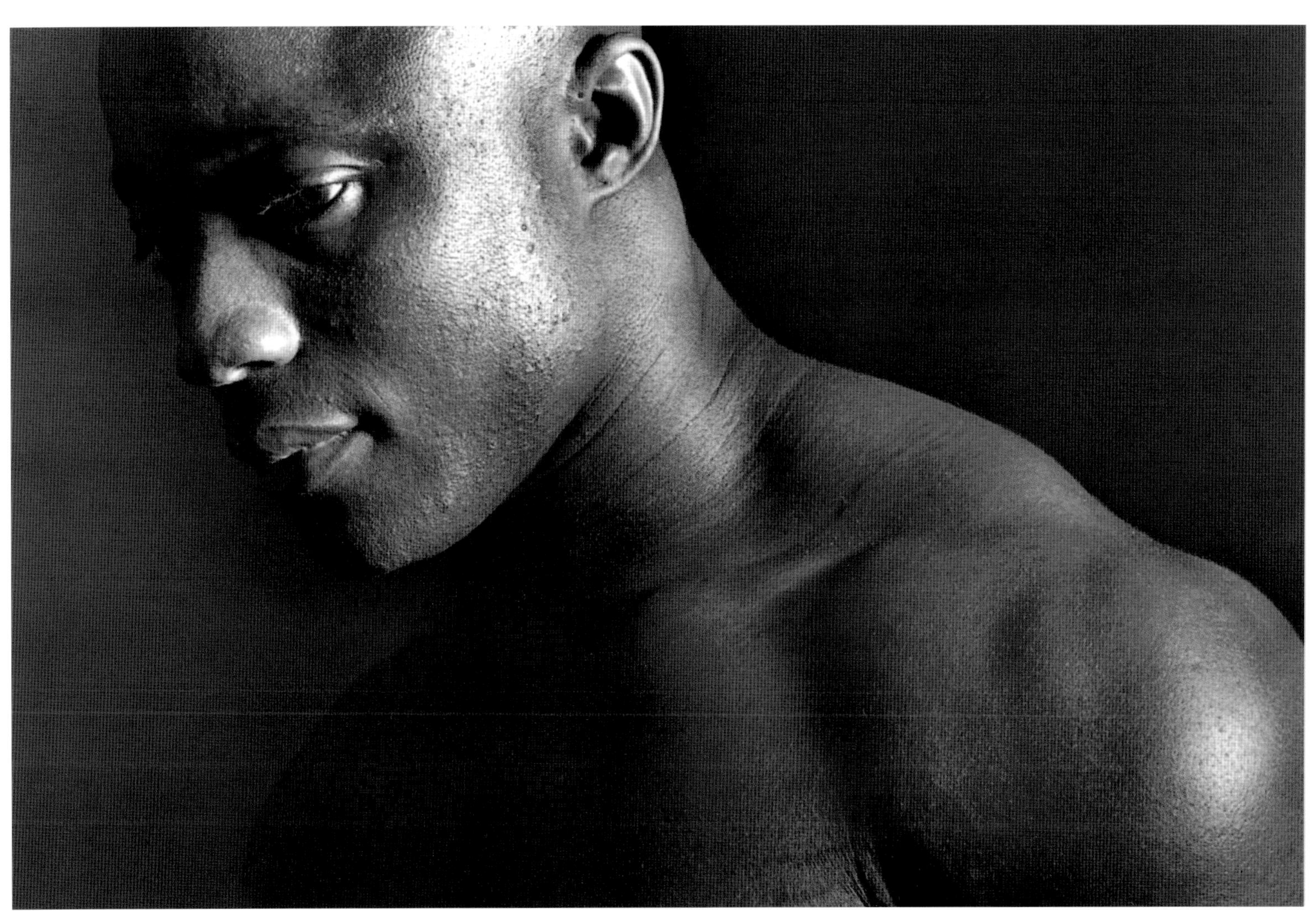

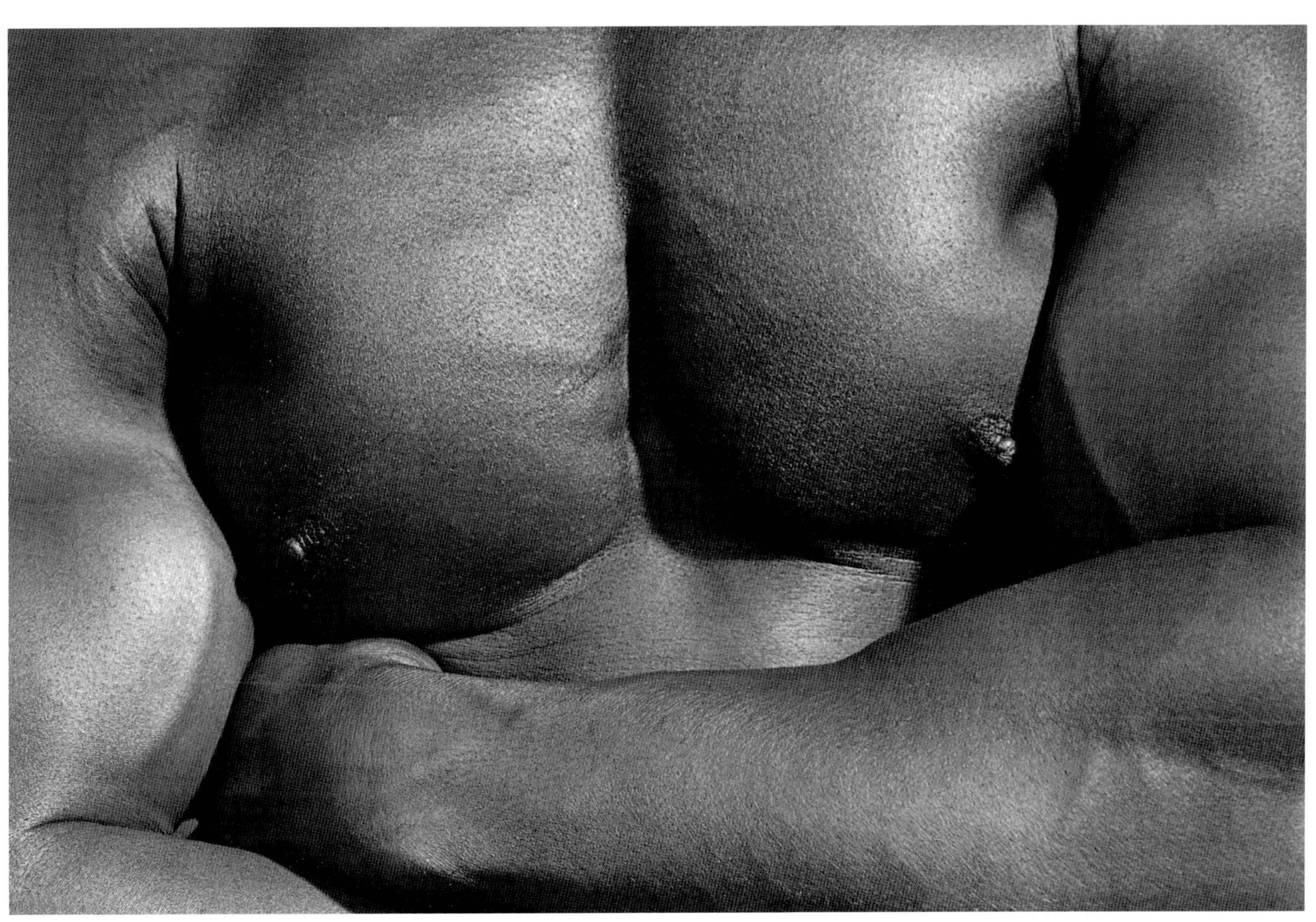

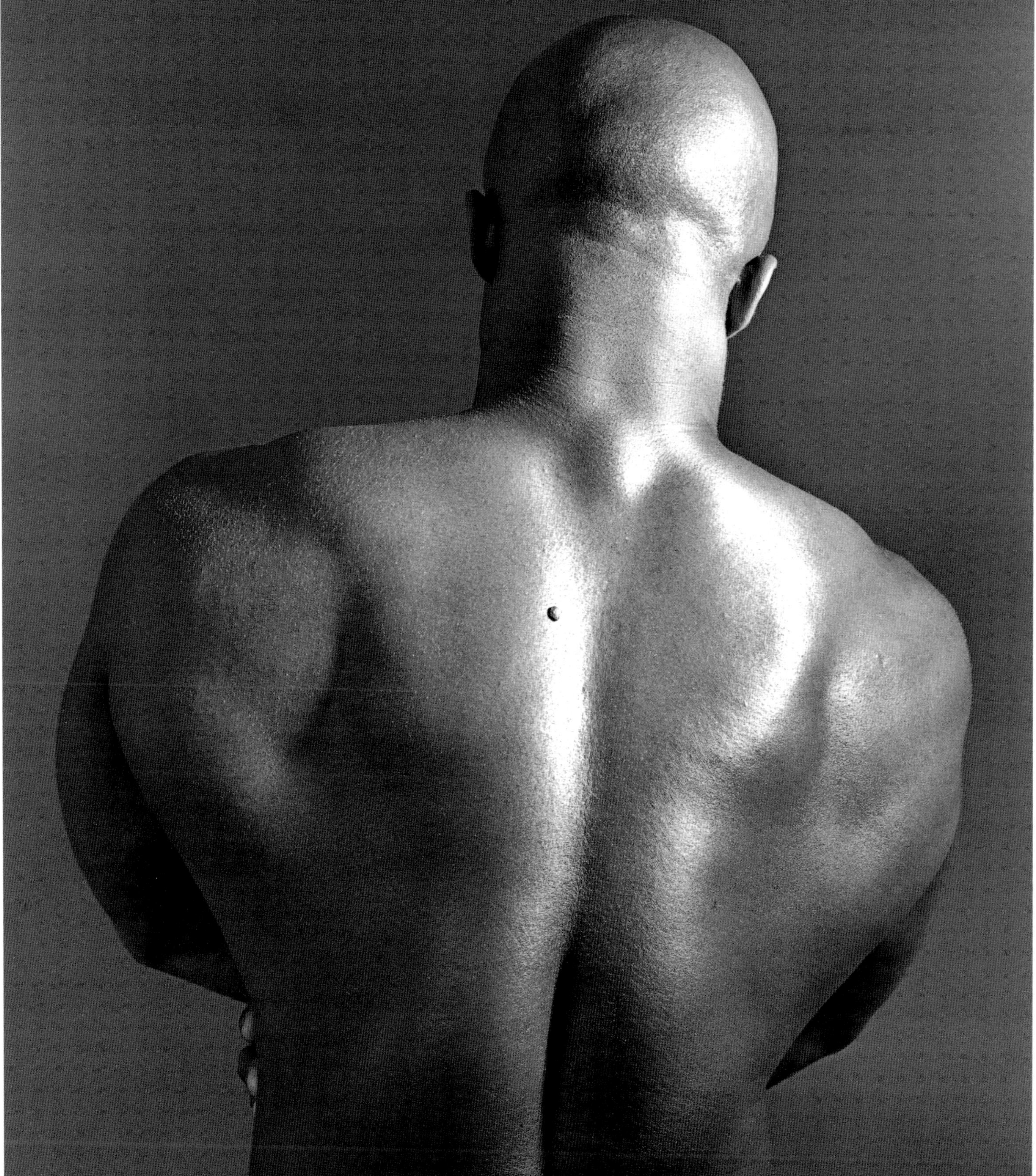

Michael on my living room sofa, Brookline, December 1998

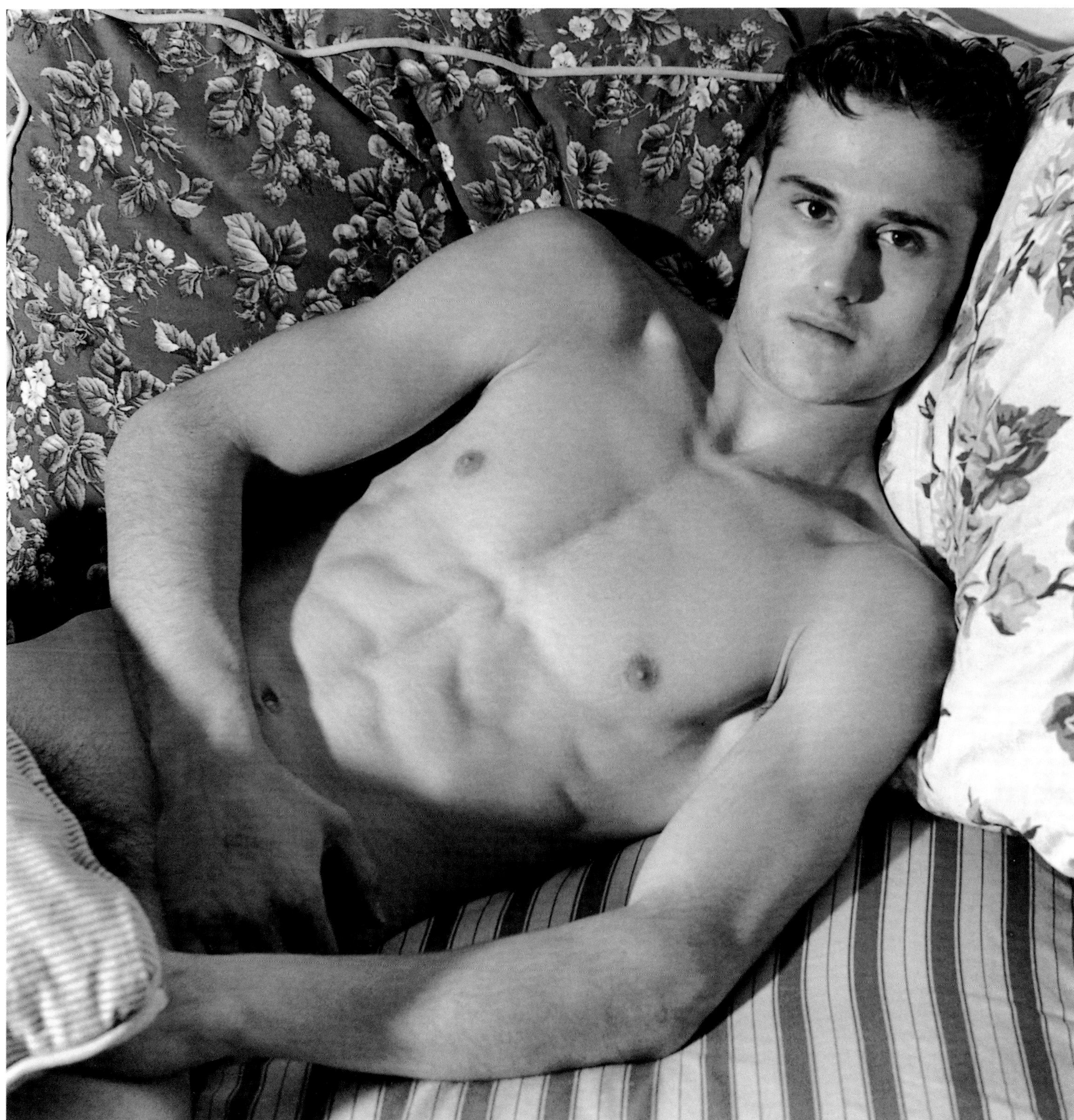

Michael in Laura Van Wormer's stairwell, Meriden, CT, December 1998

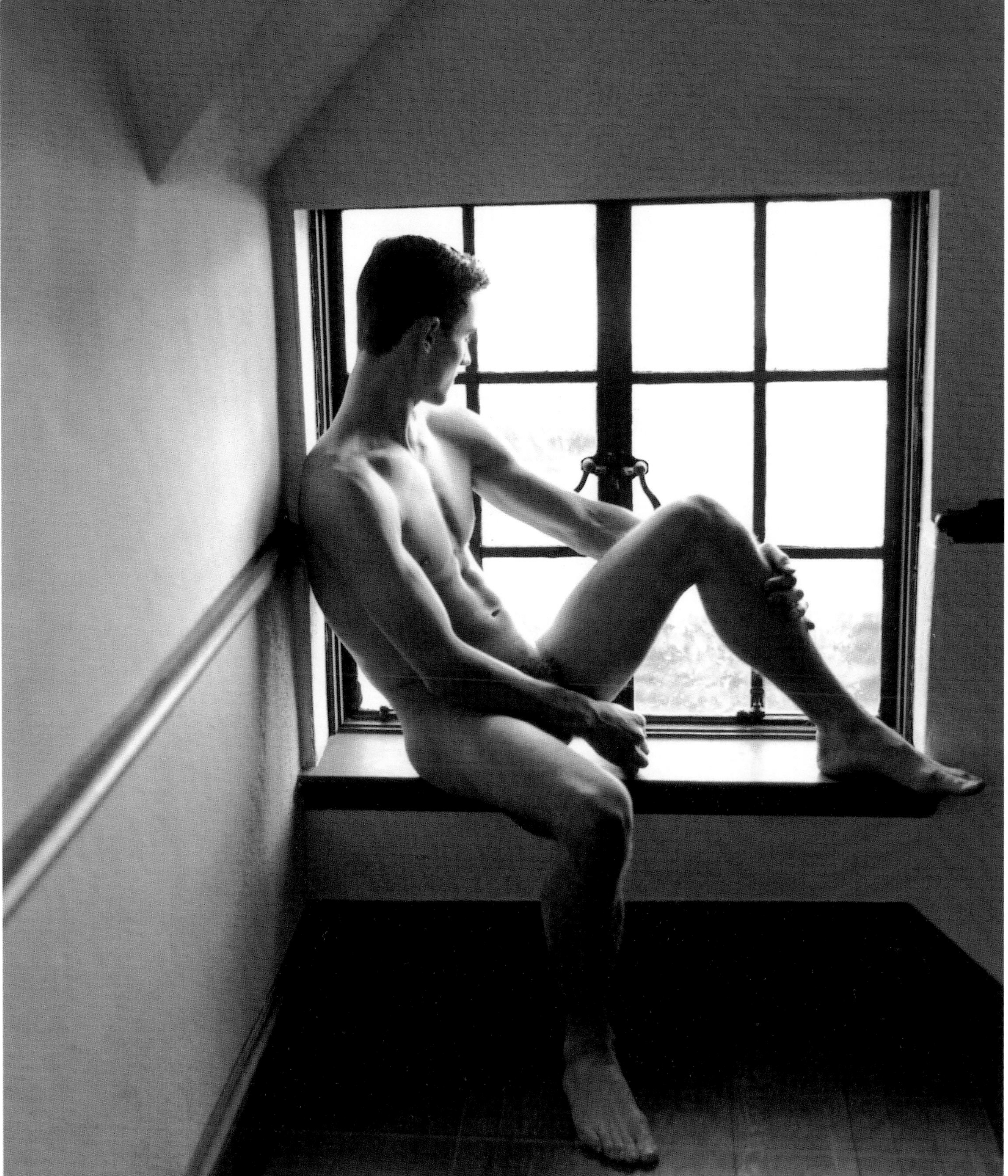

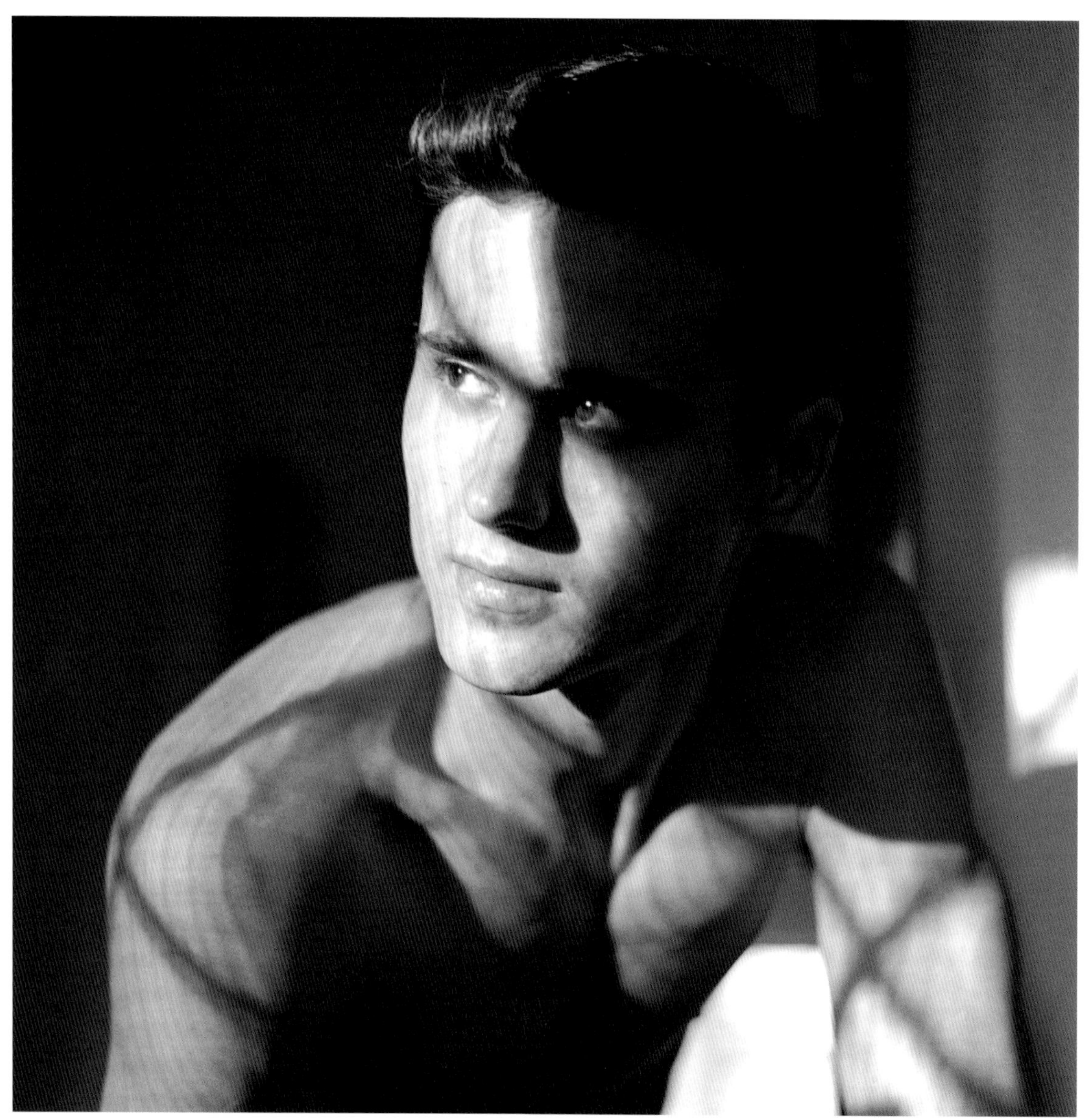

Michael in Laura Van Wormer's living room, Meriden, December 1998

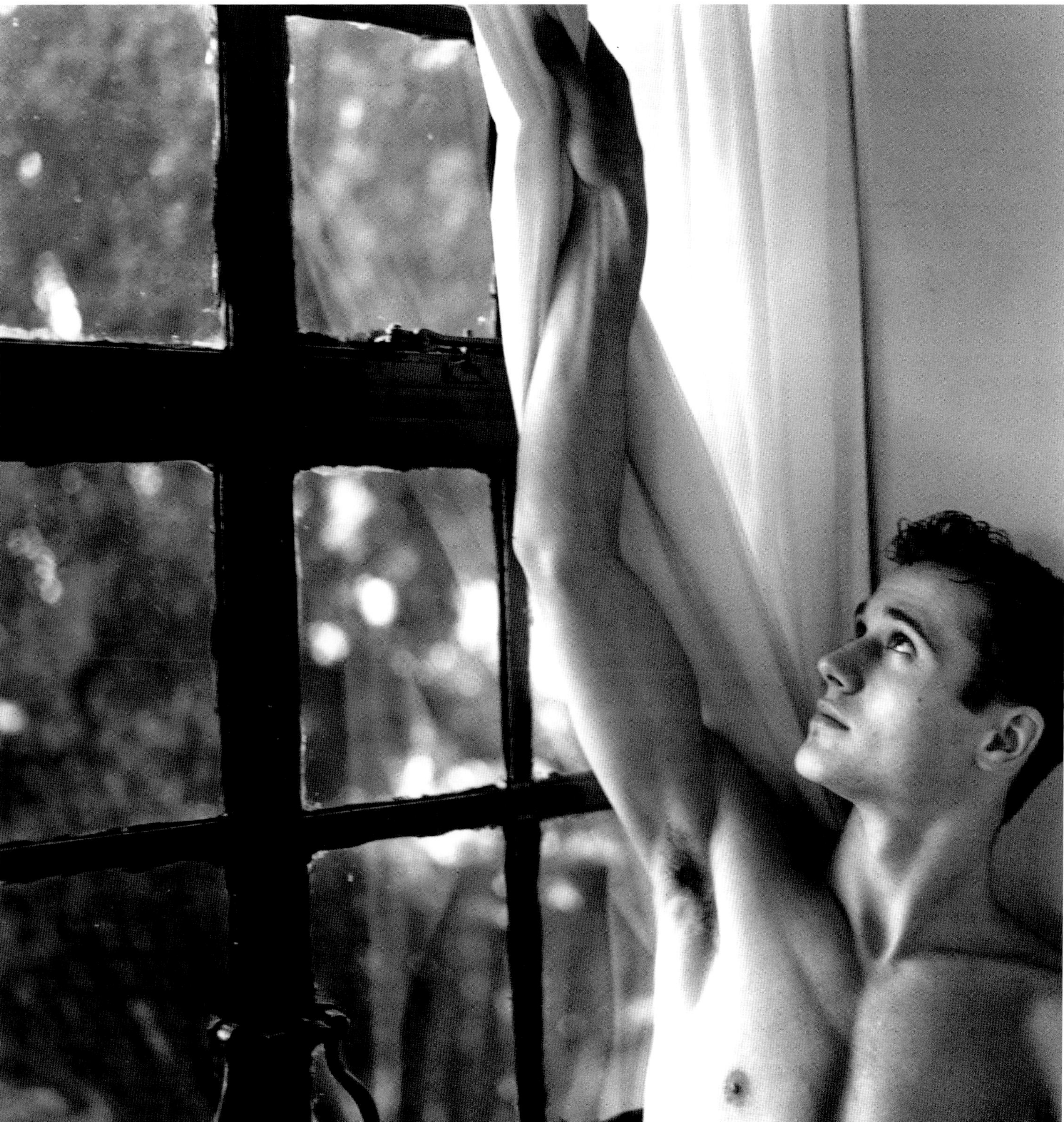

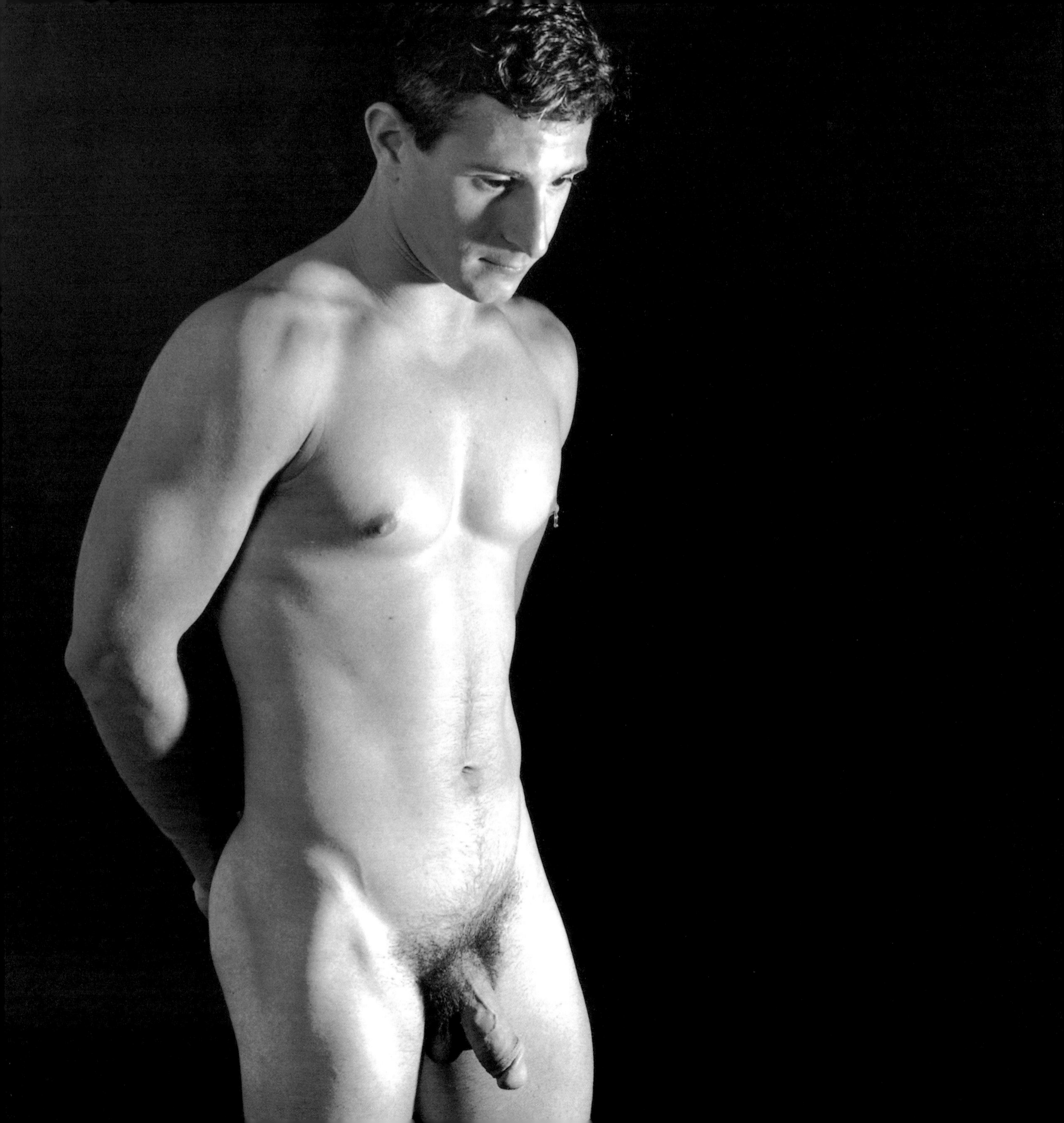

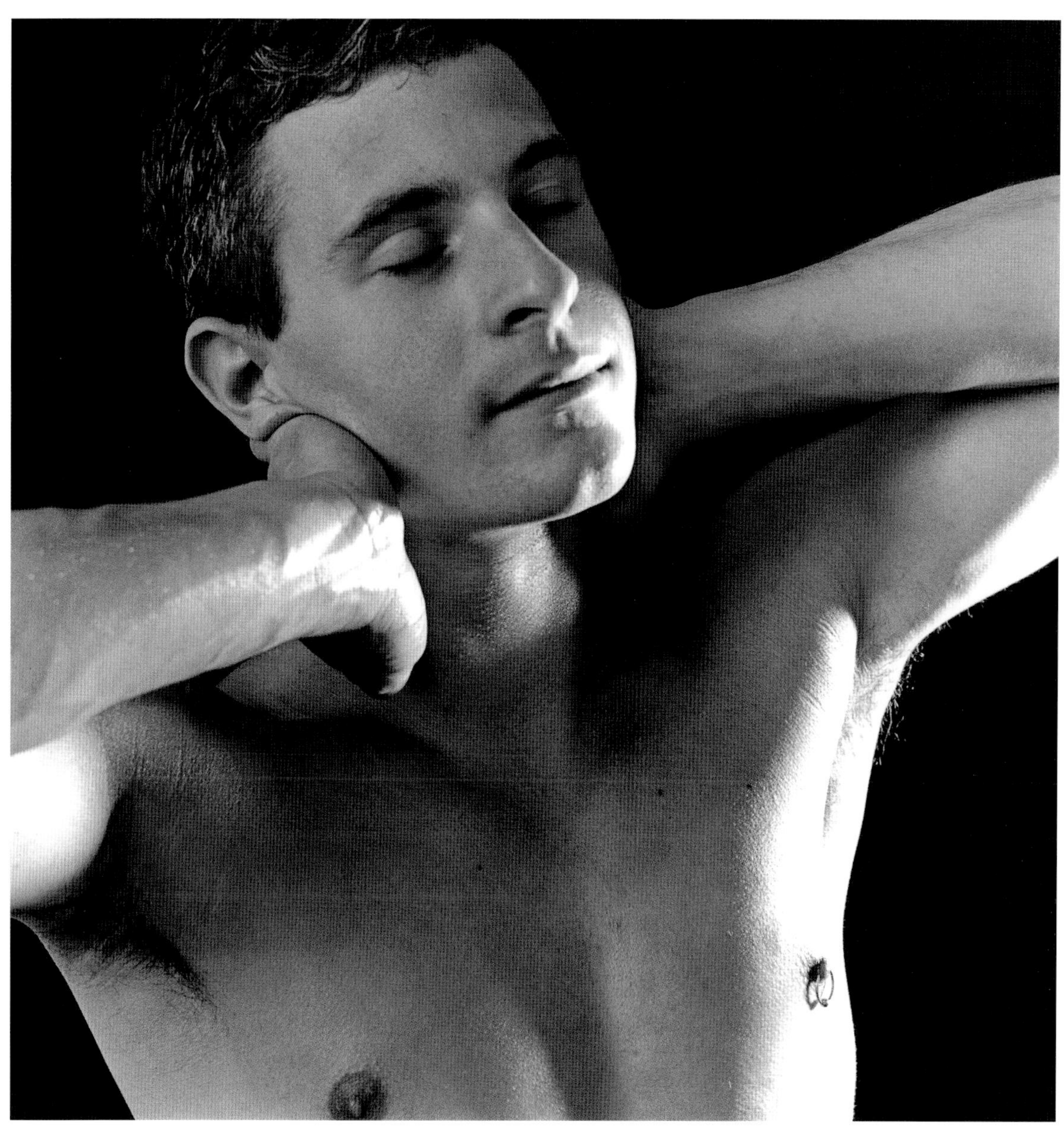

David in my studio, Brookline, August 1998

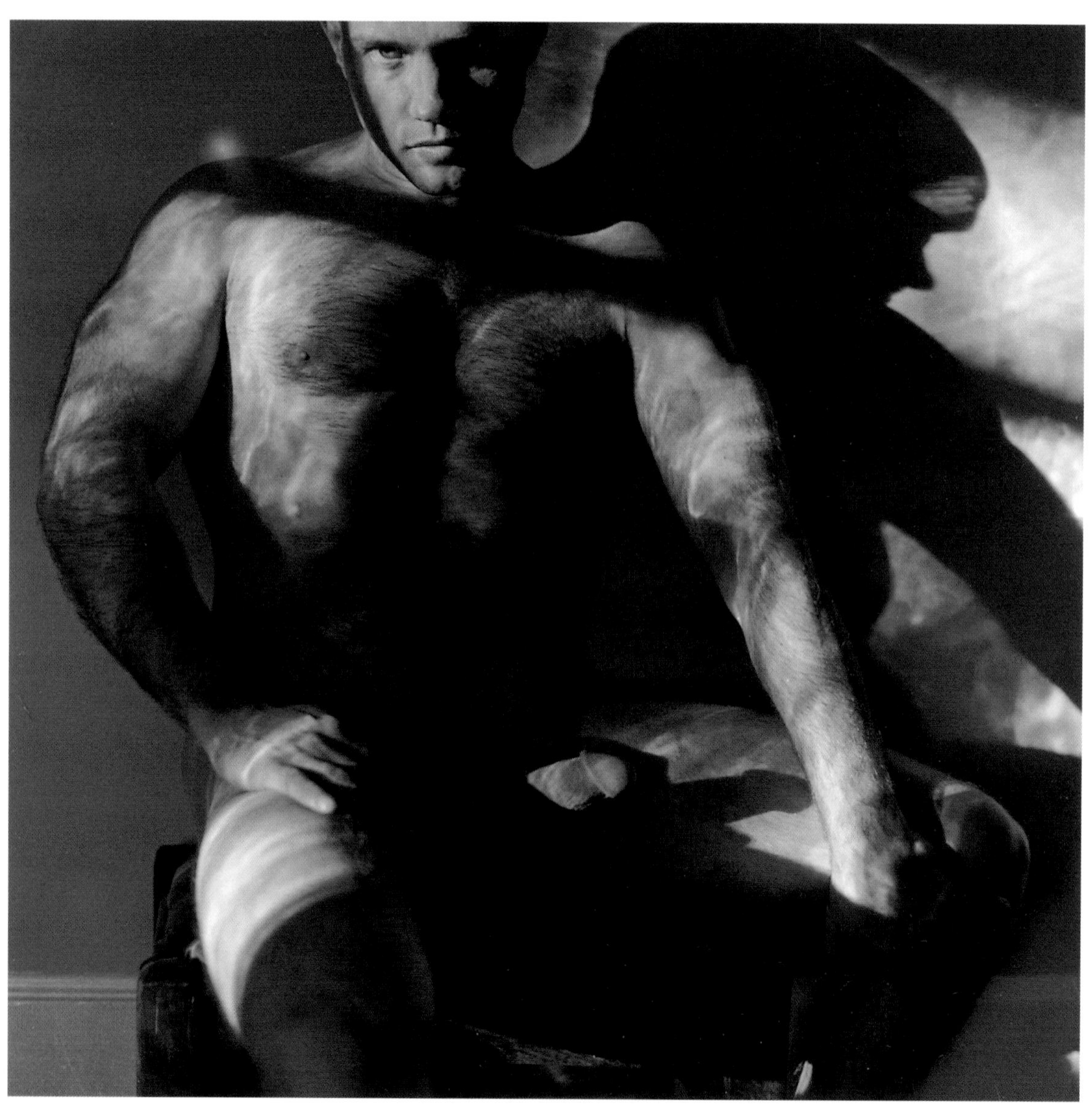

Andre in my den, Natick, MA, December 1999

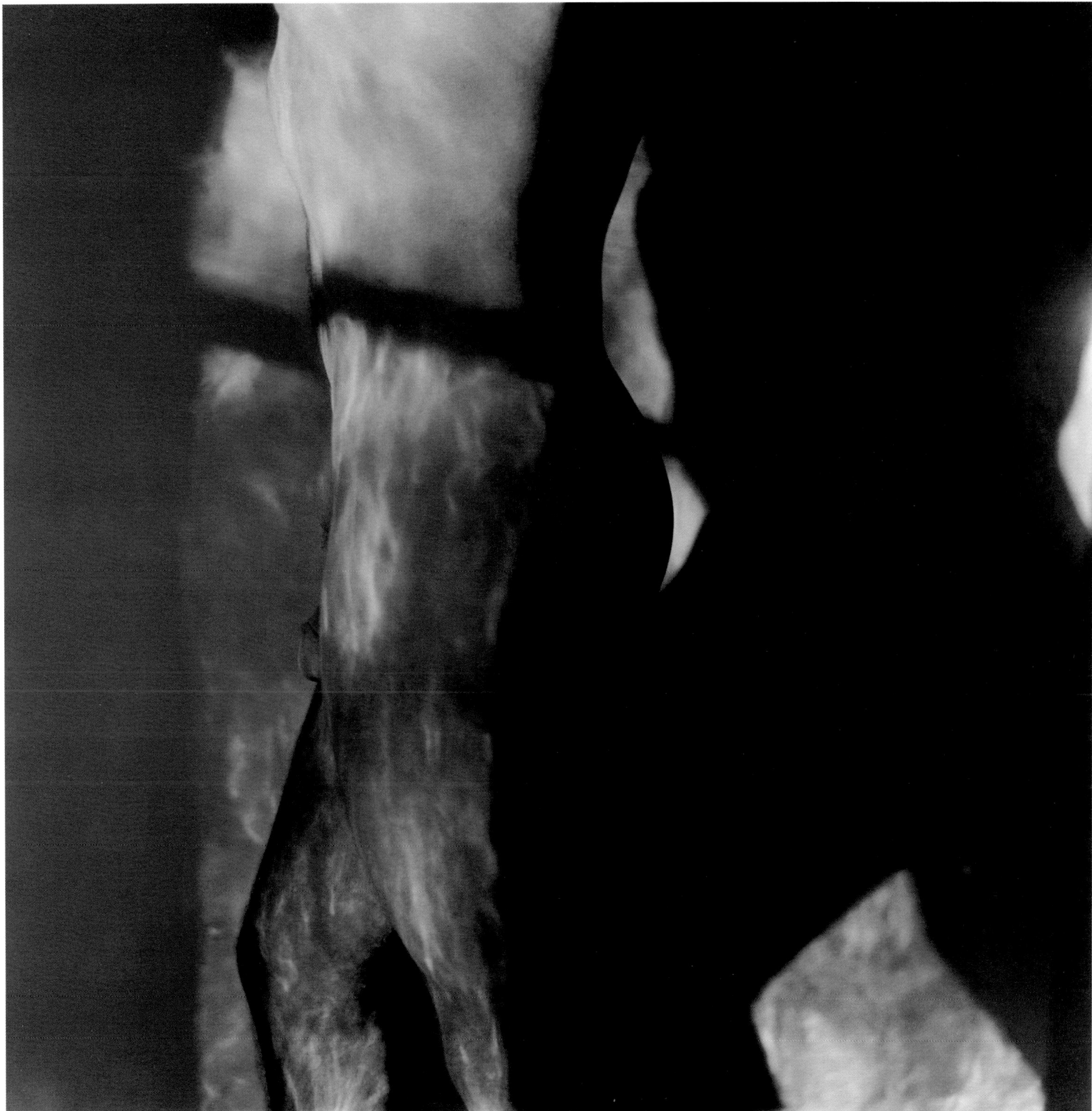

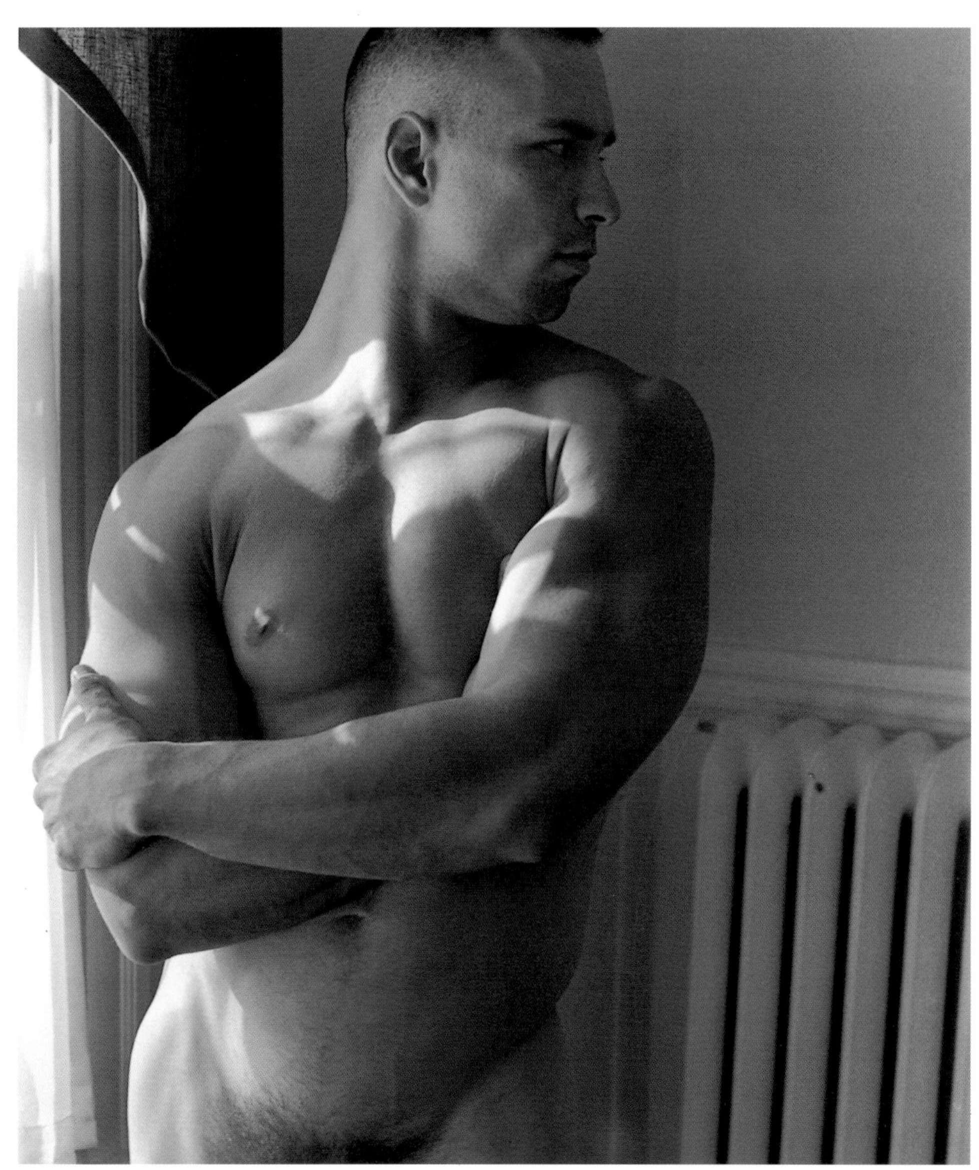

Tom in my studio, Brookline, November 1998

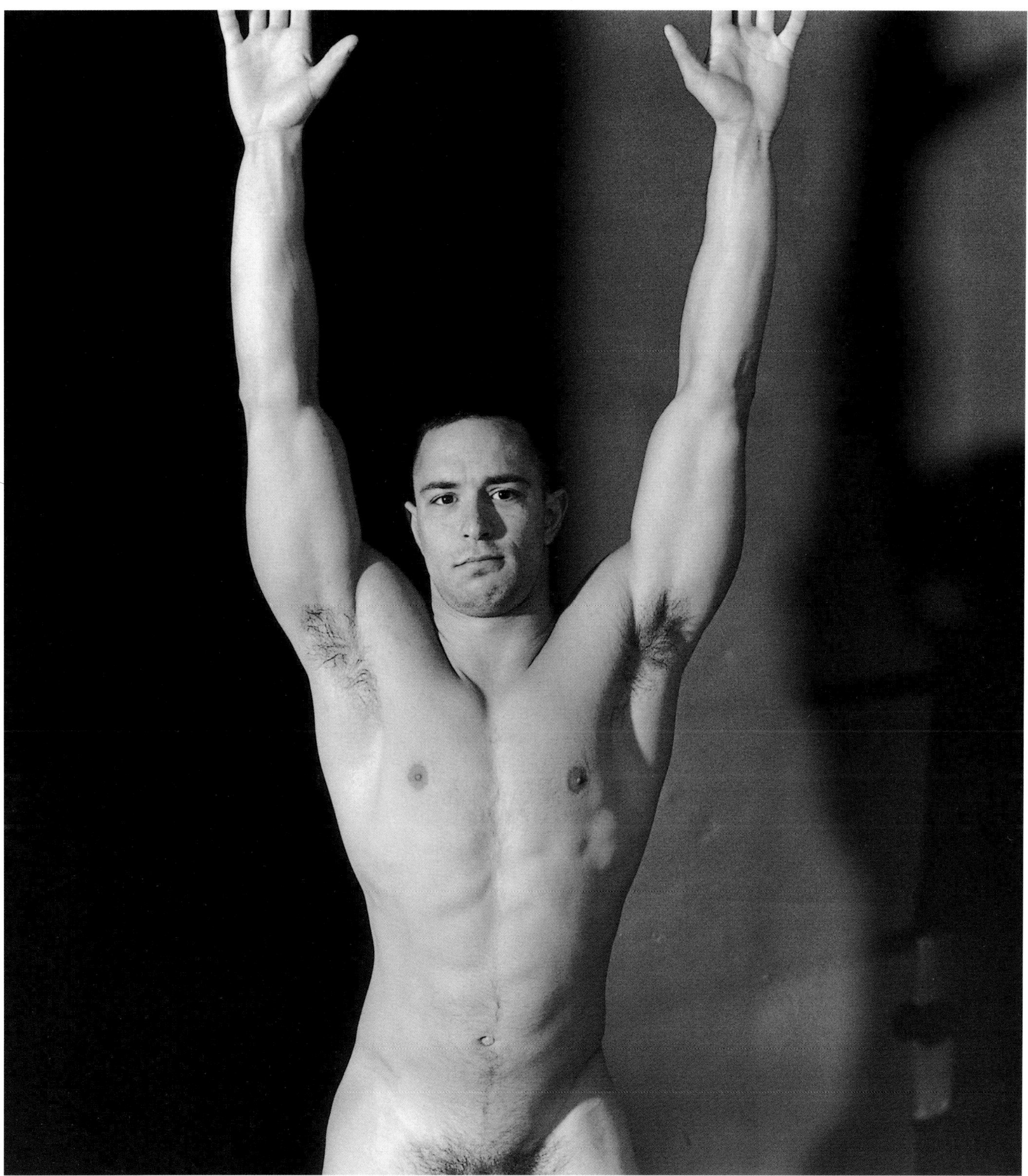

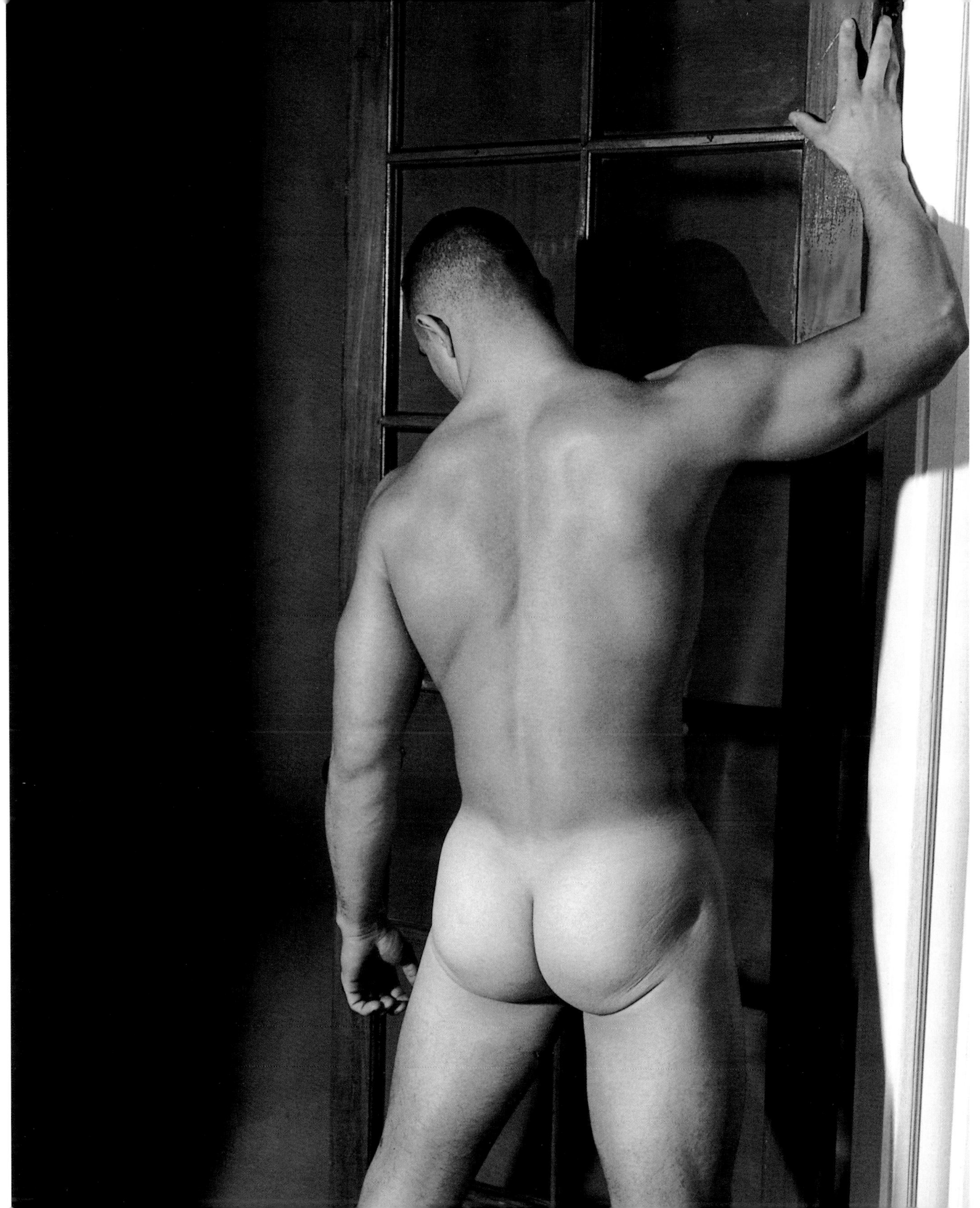

Paul in my studio, Brookline, July 1998

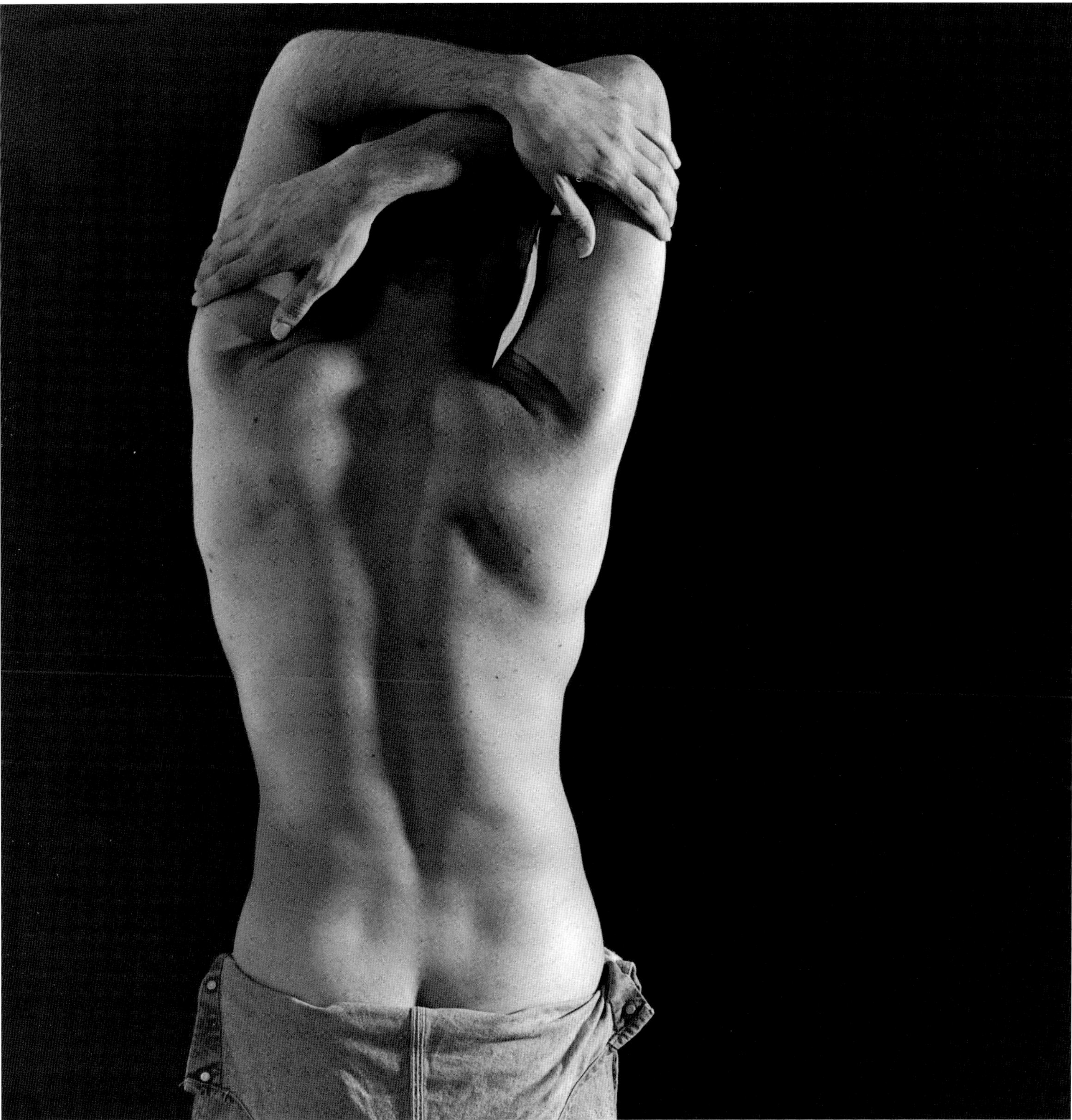

Eldred in my living room, Brookline, December 1998

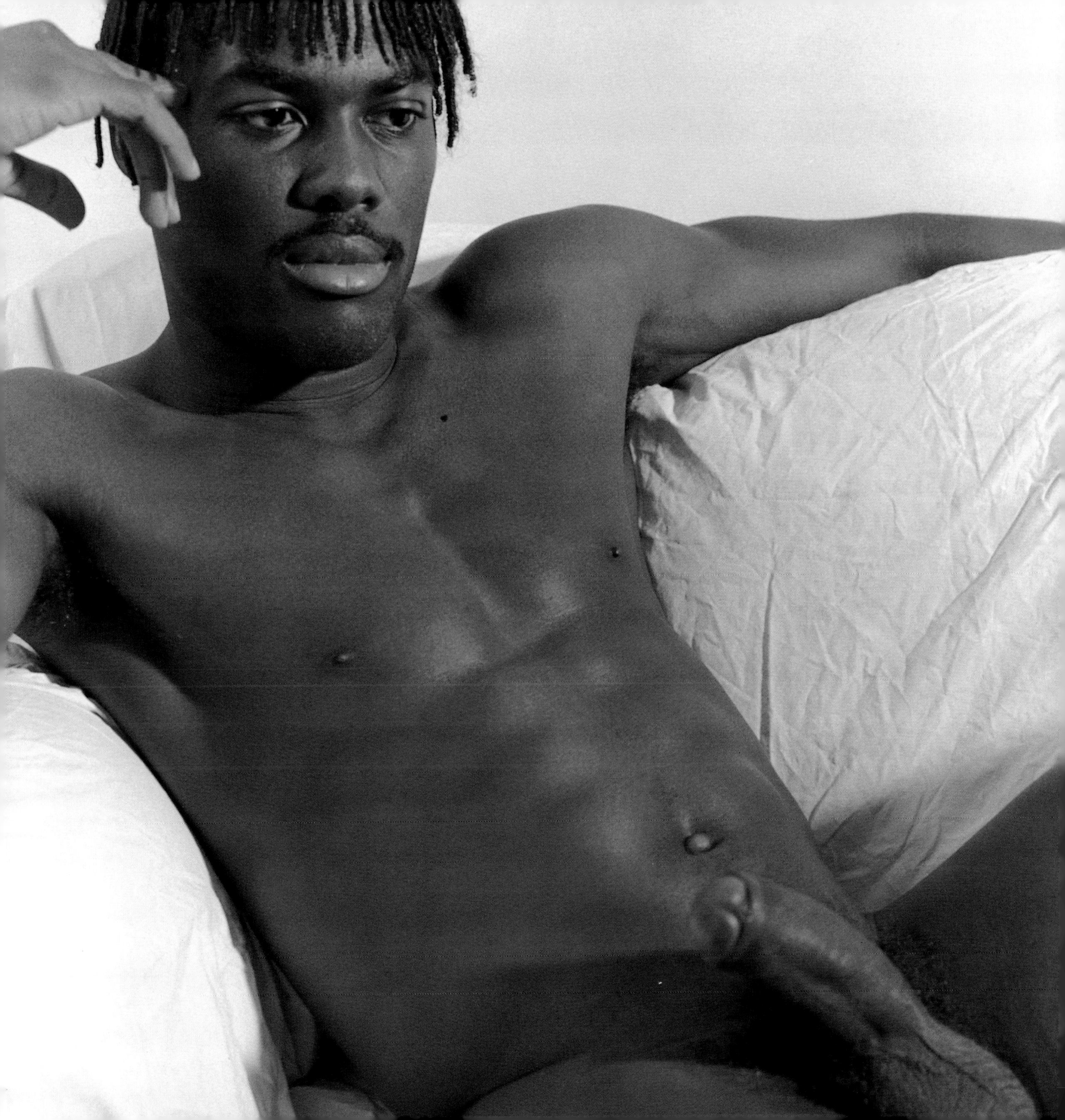

44

Spencer in my studio, Brookline, February 1998

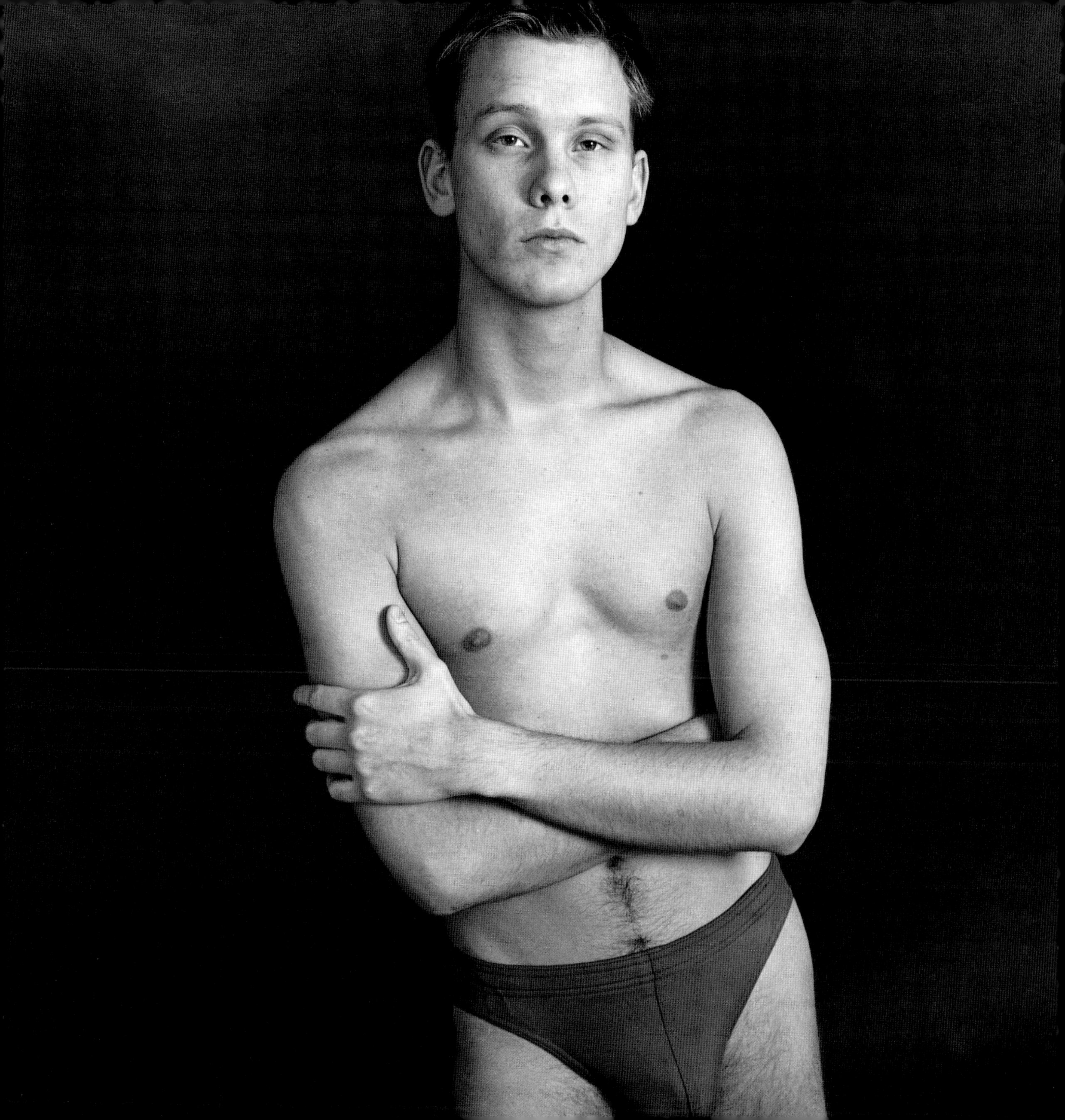

Spencer in my basement, Brookline, June 1998

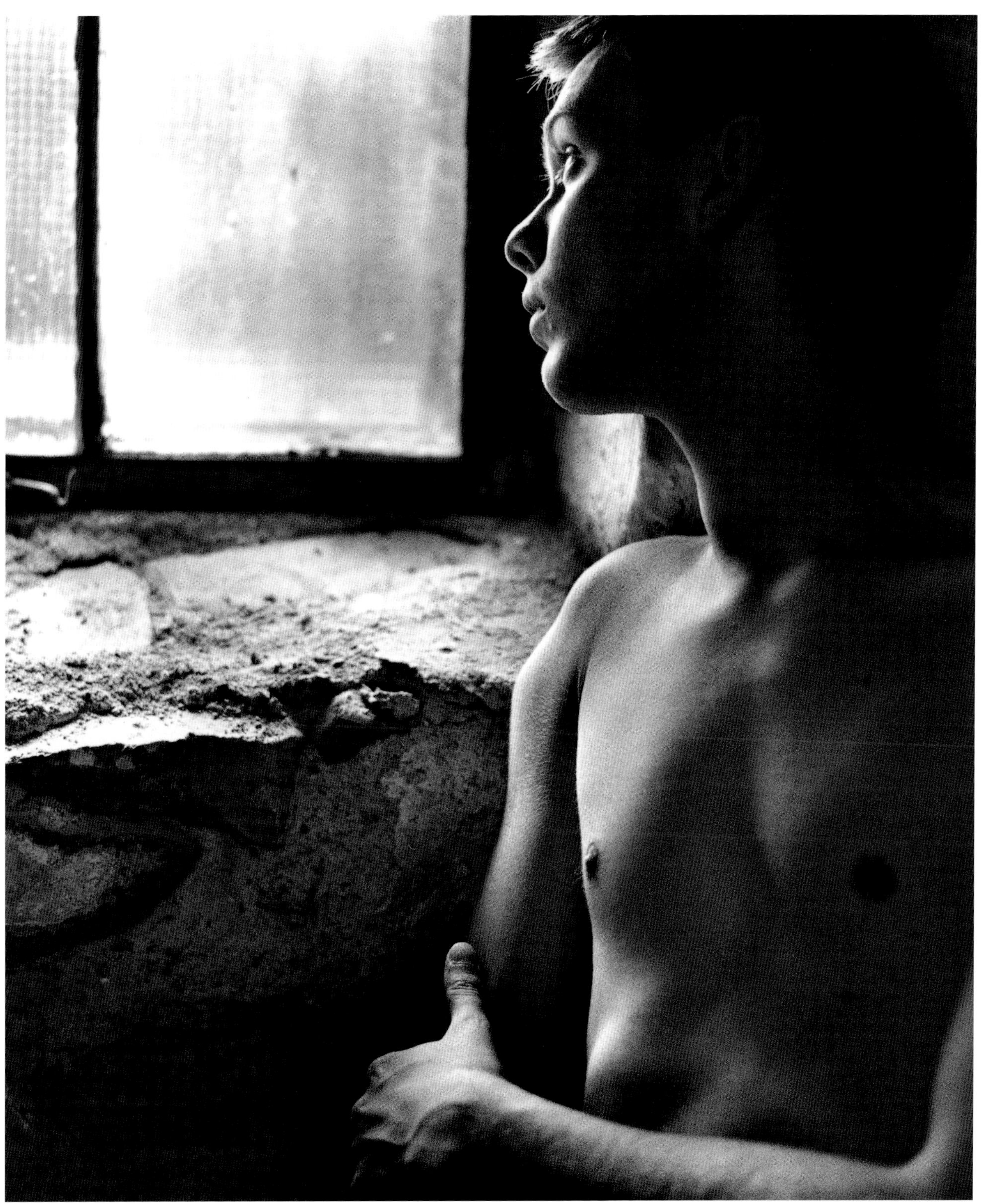

Spencer in my studio, Brookline, February 1998

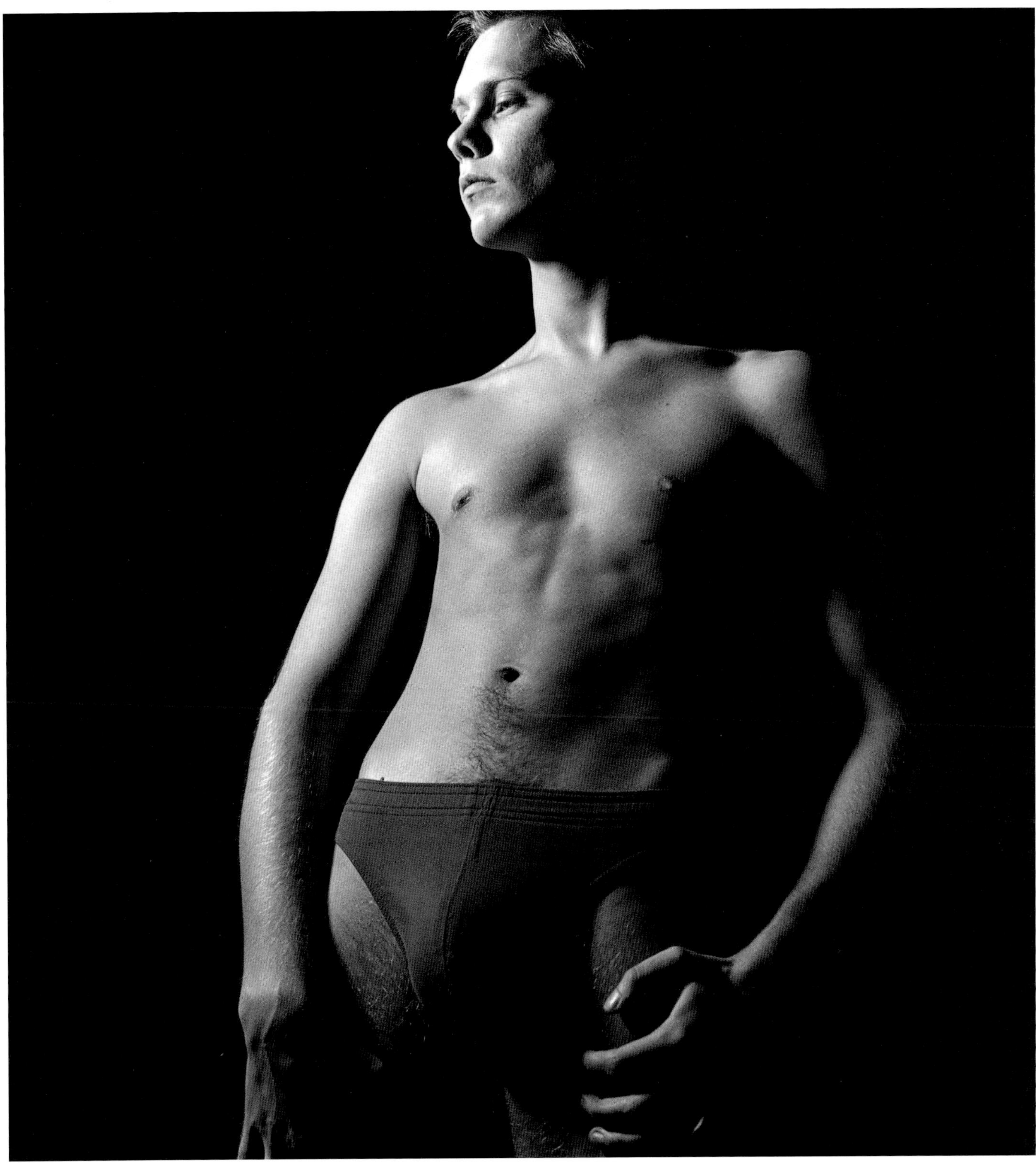

50

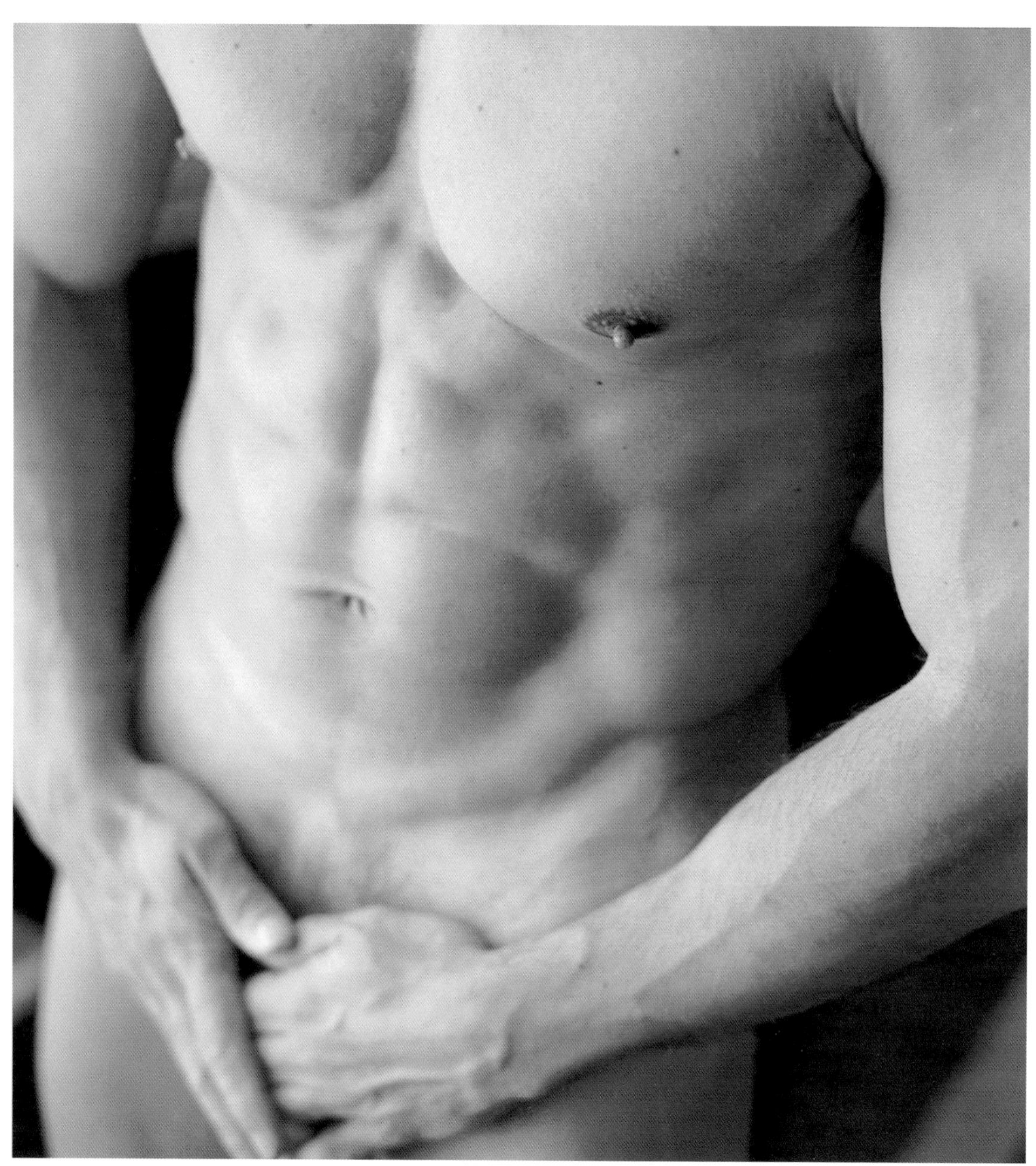

Scott in my dining room, Natick, December 1999

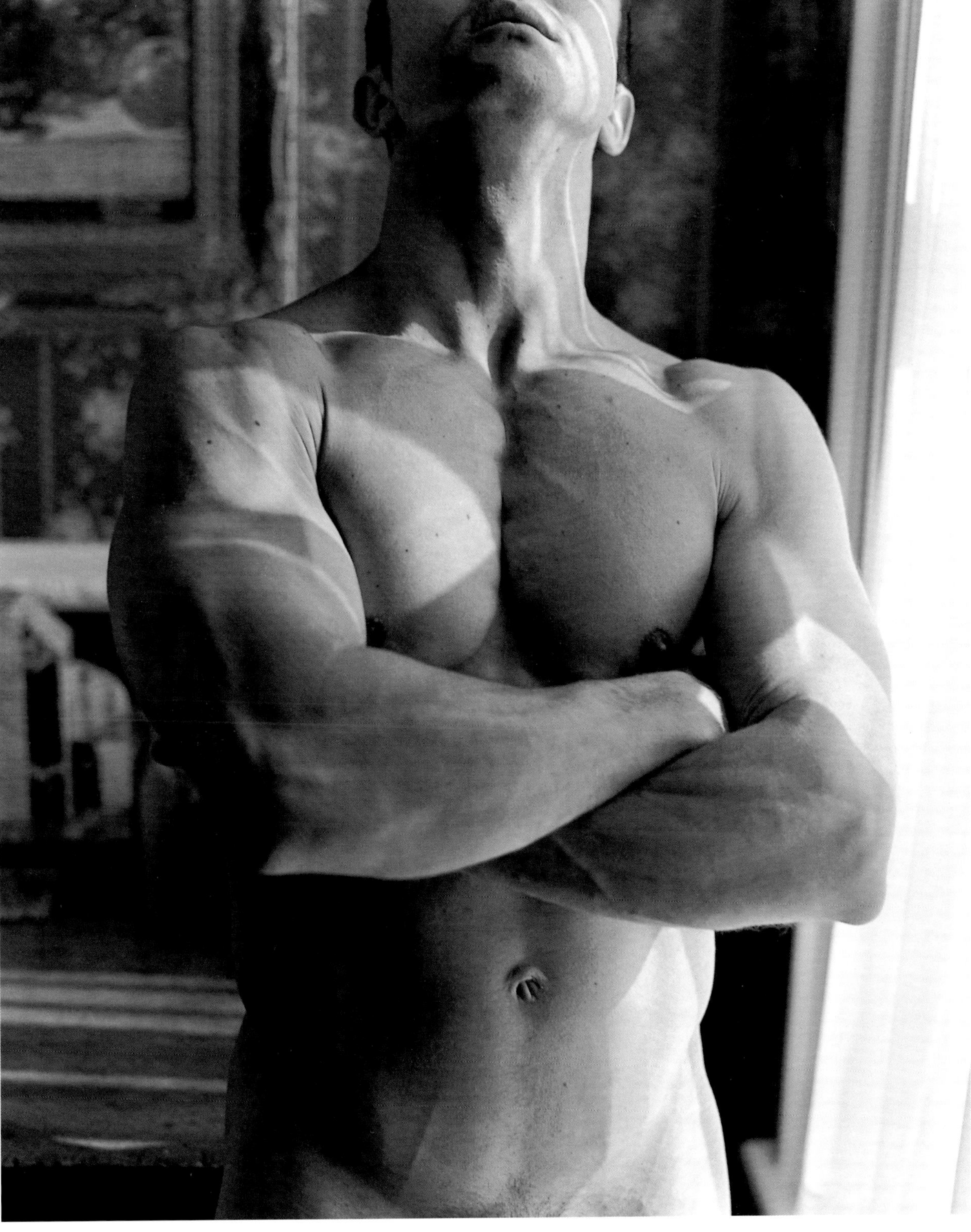

Sean in my studio, Brookline, January 1998

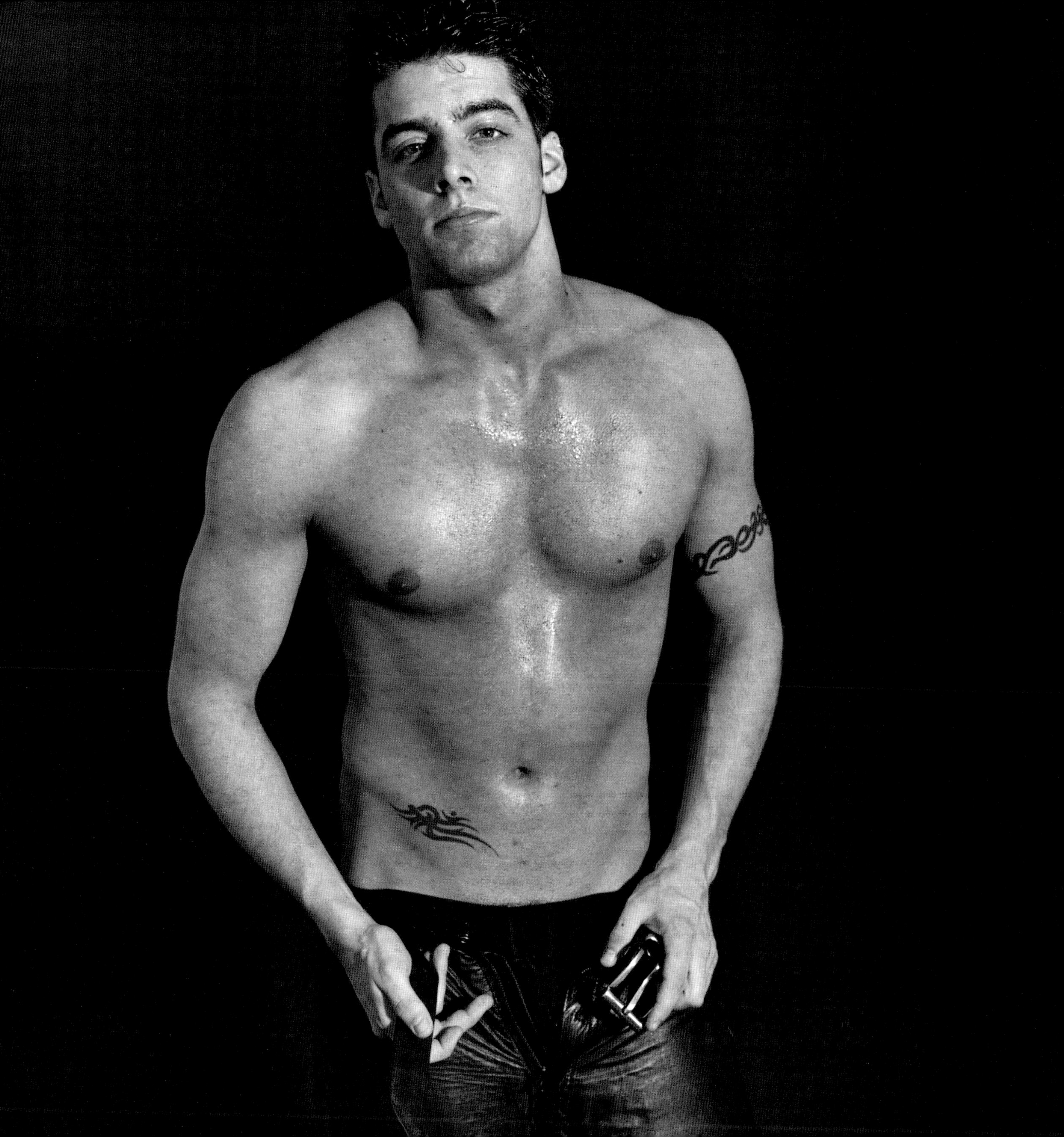

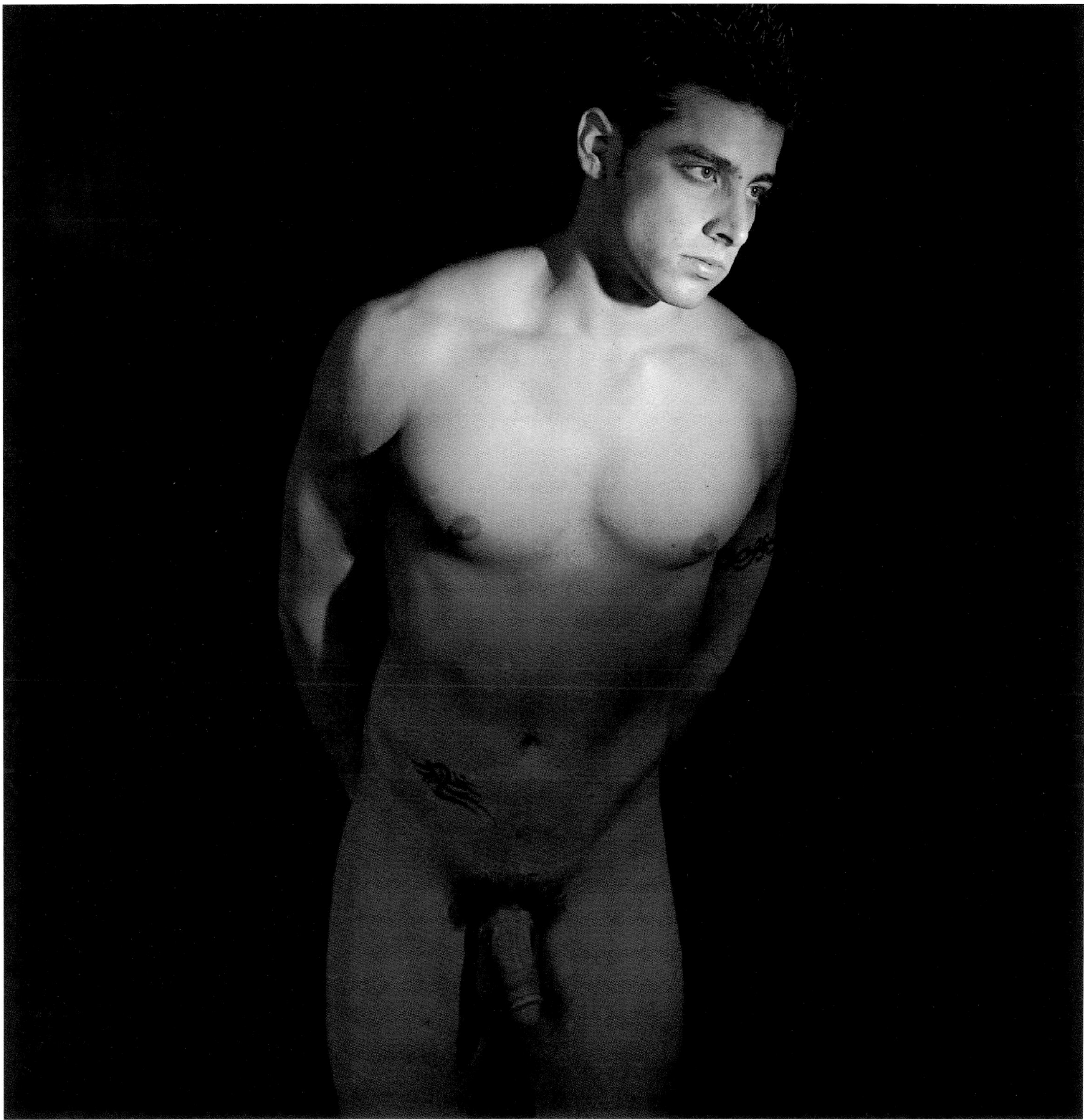

Sean in my living room, Brookline, November 1998

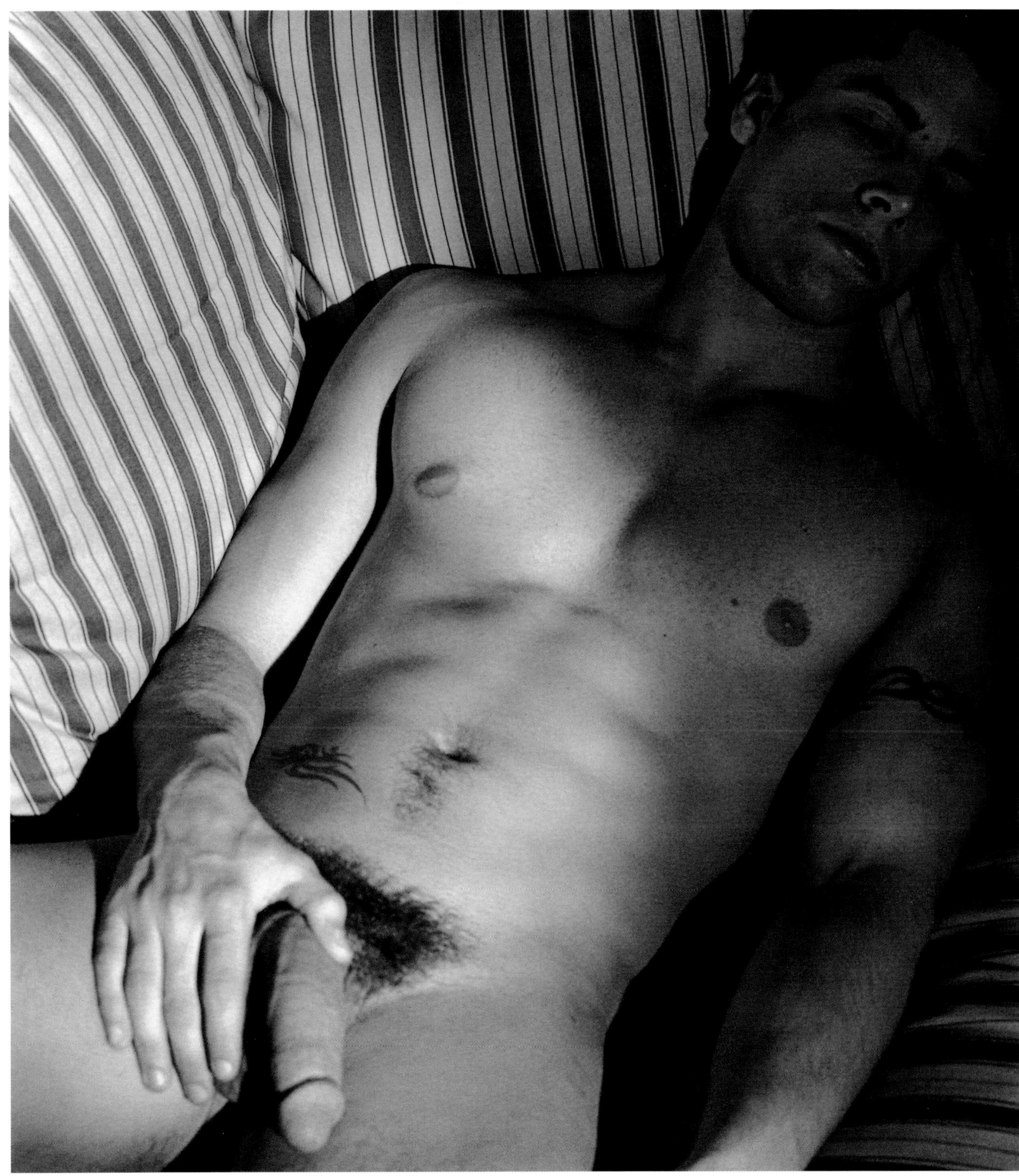

Drew in my studio, Brookline, December 1998

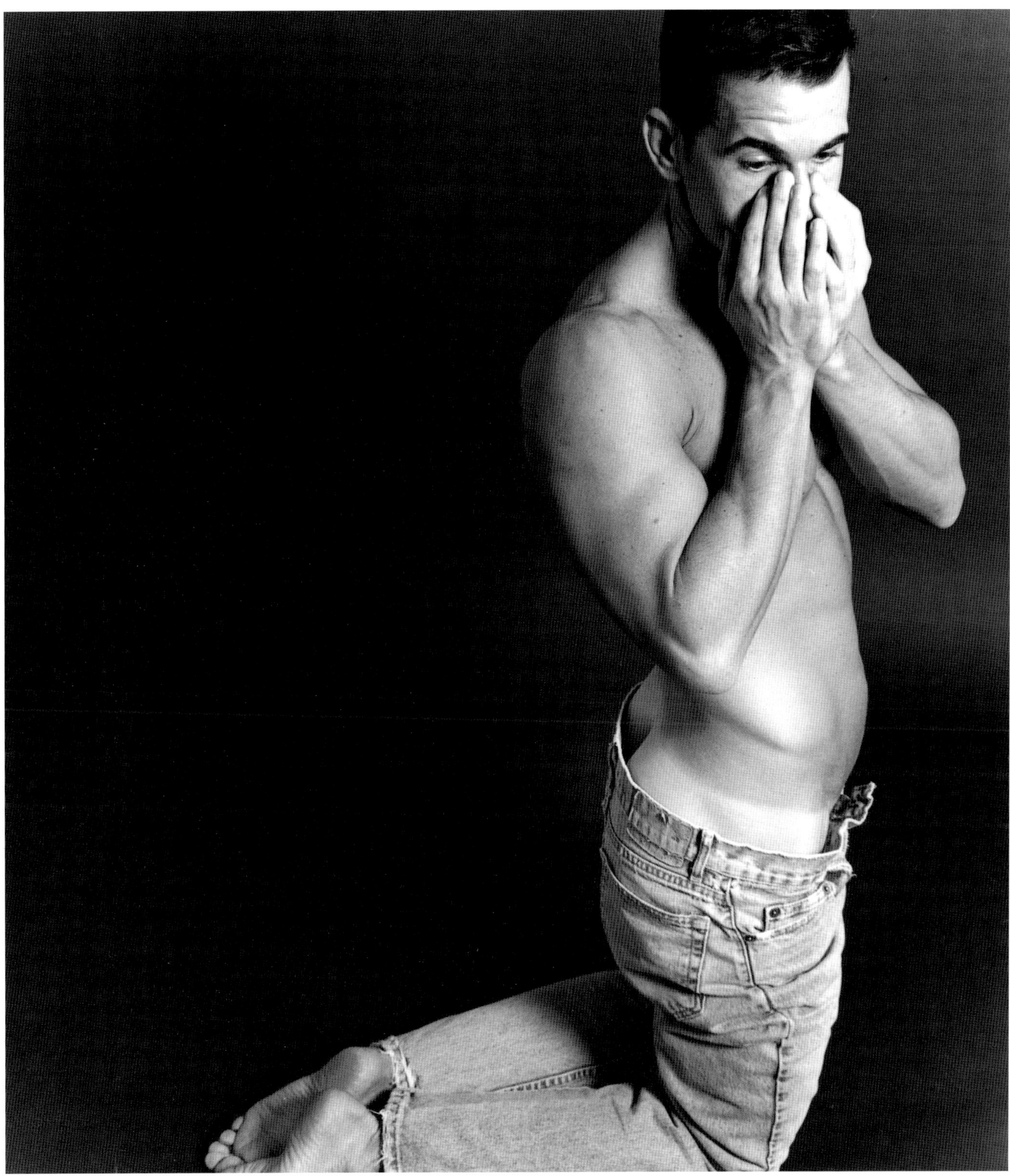

Terrance in my dining room, Brookline, January 1999

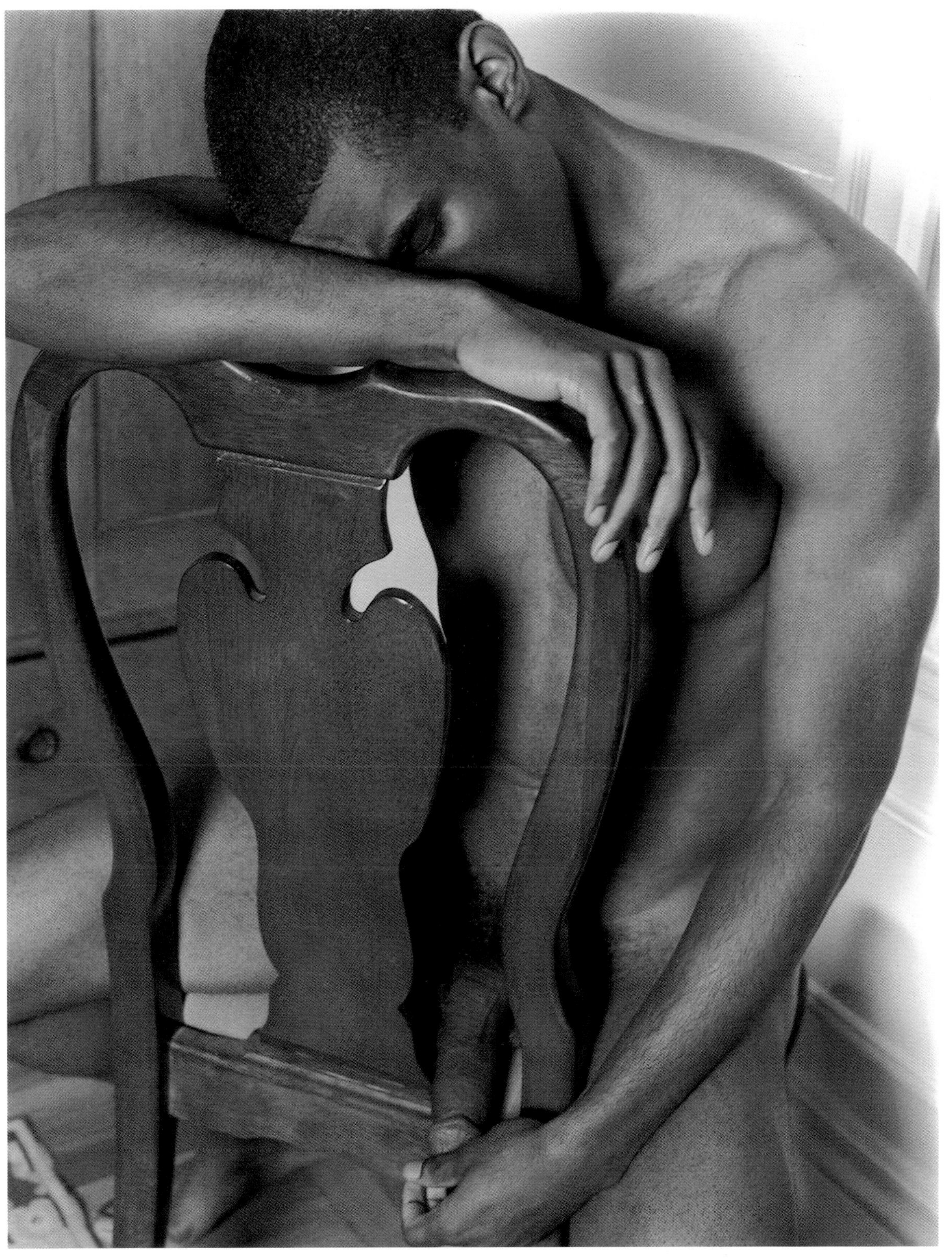

Don in Jonathan O'Leary's studio, Boston, December 1999

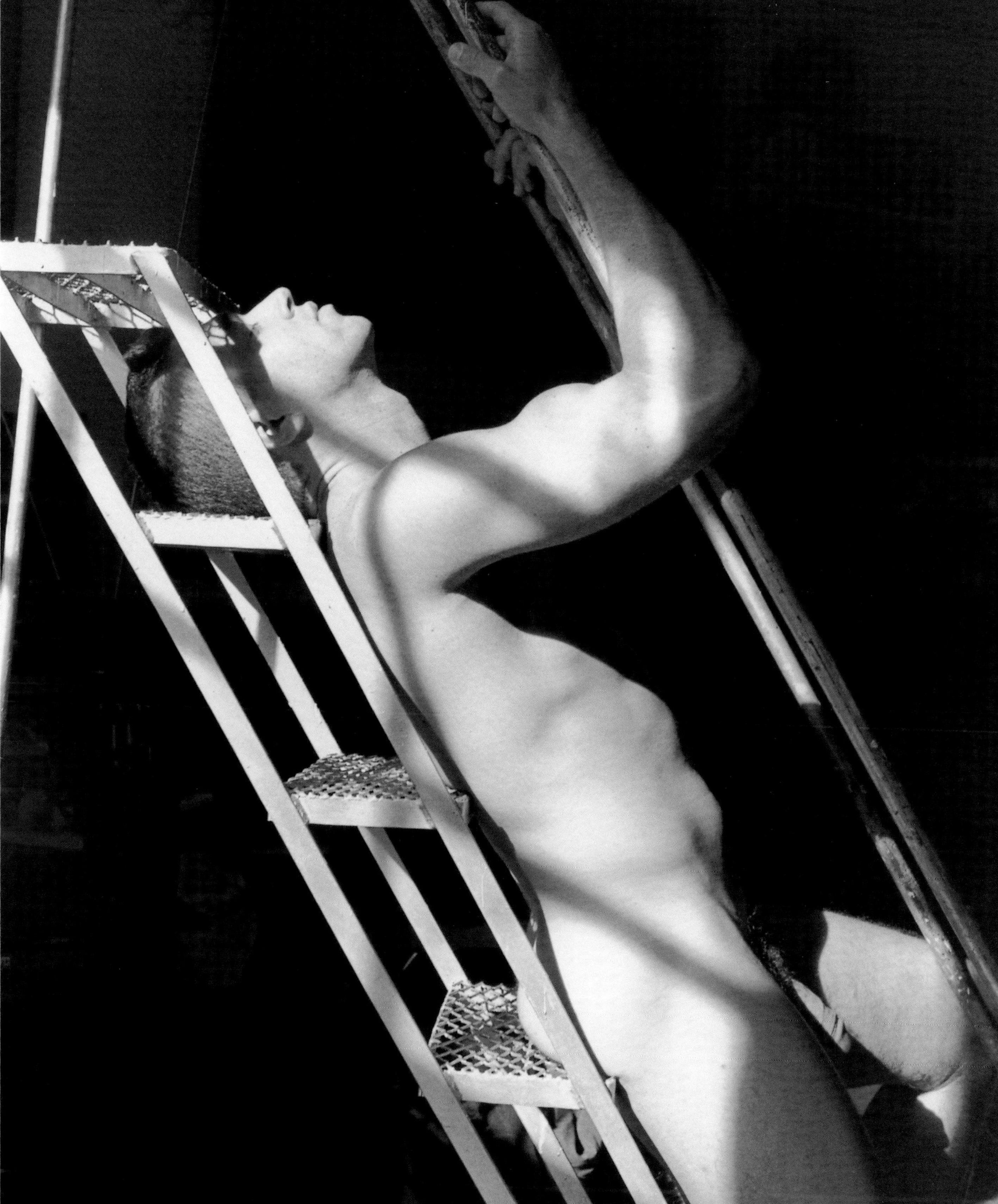

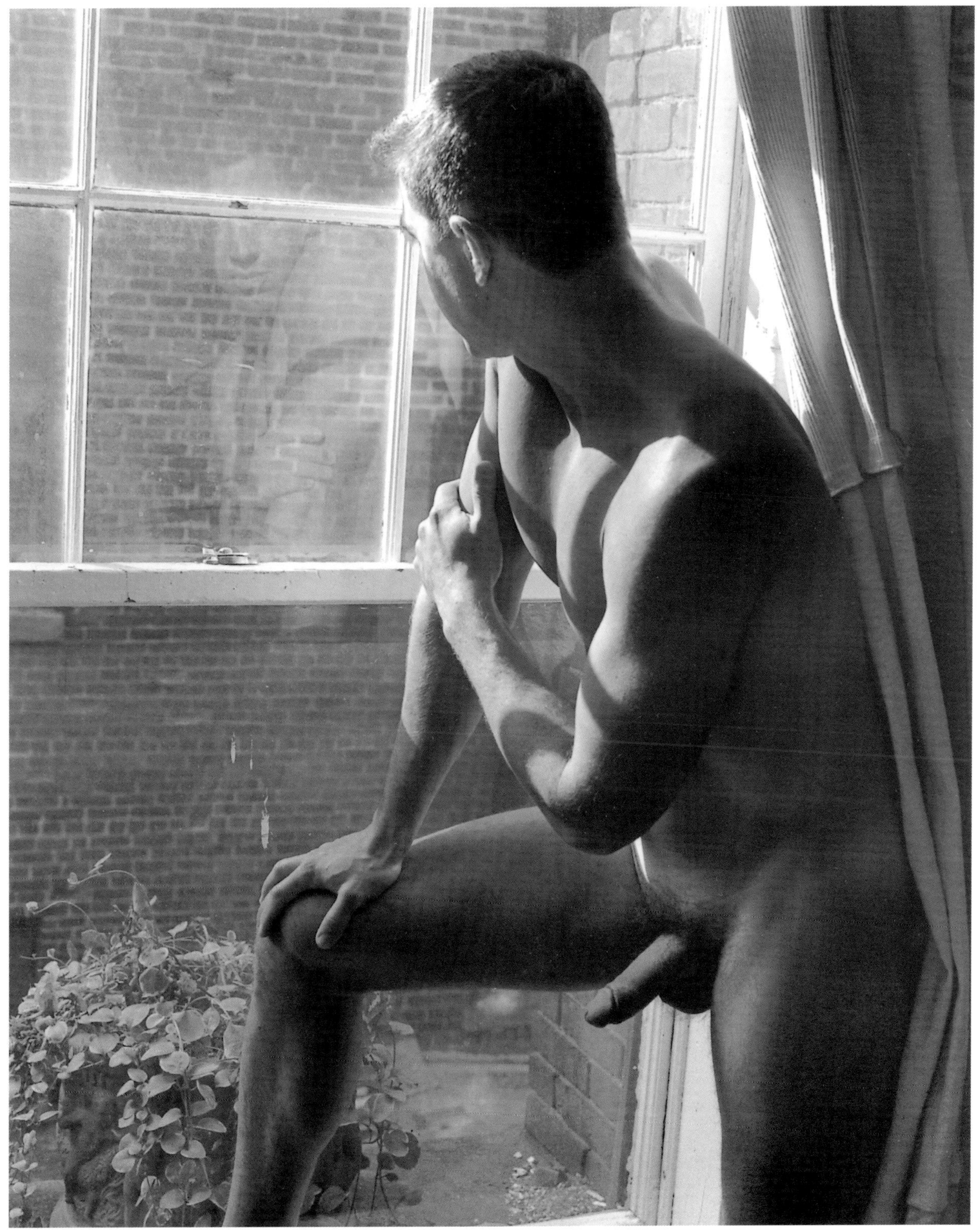

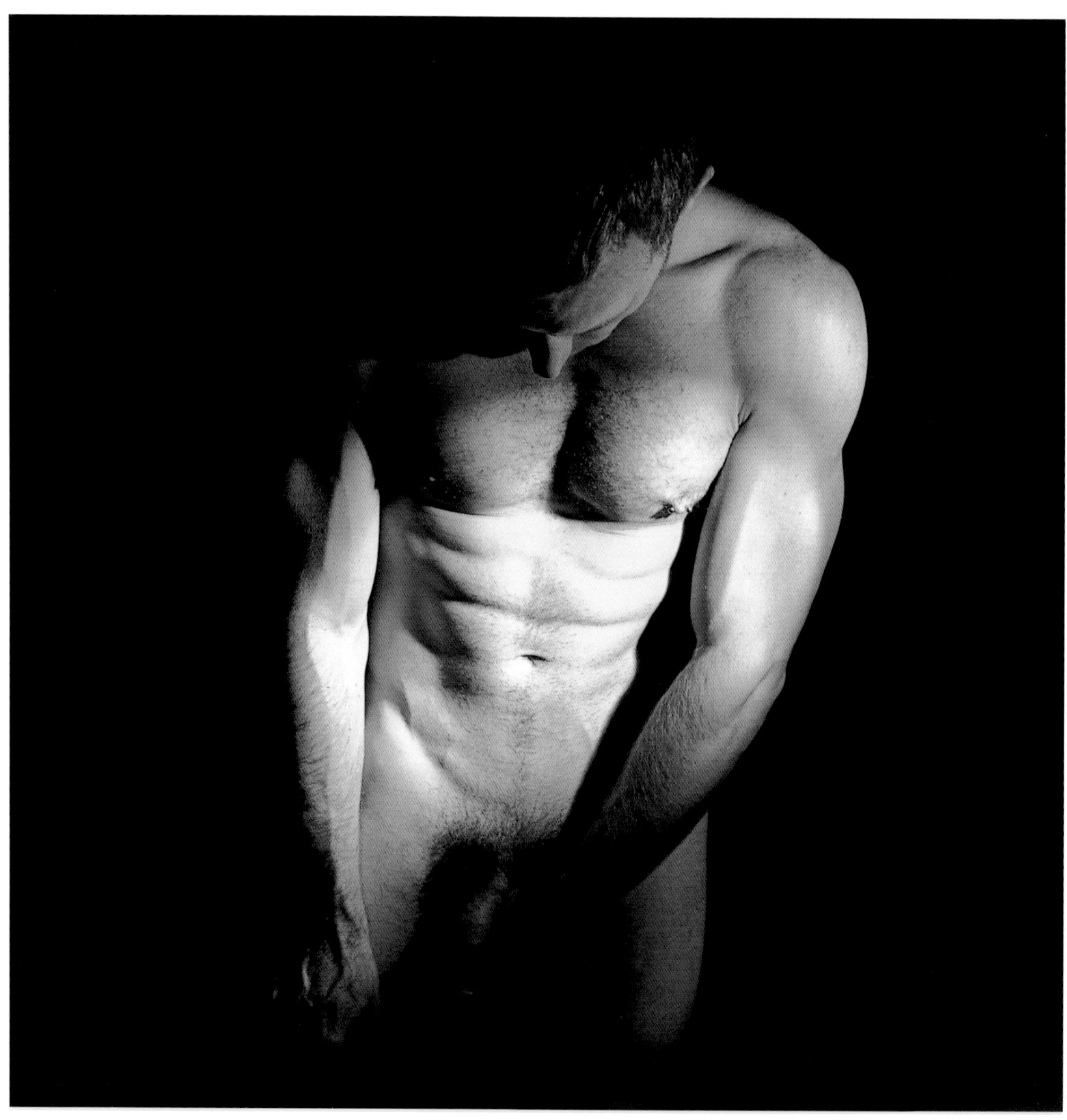

Dave in my studio, Brookline, November 1998

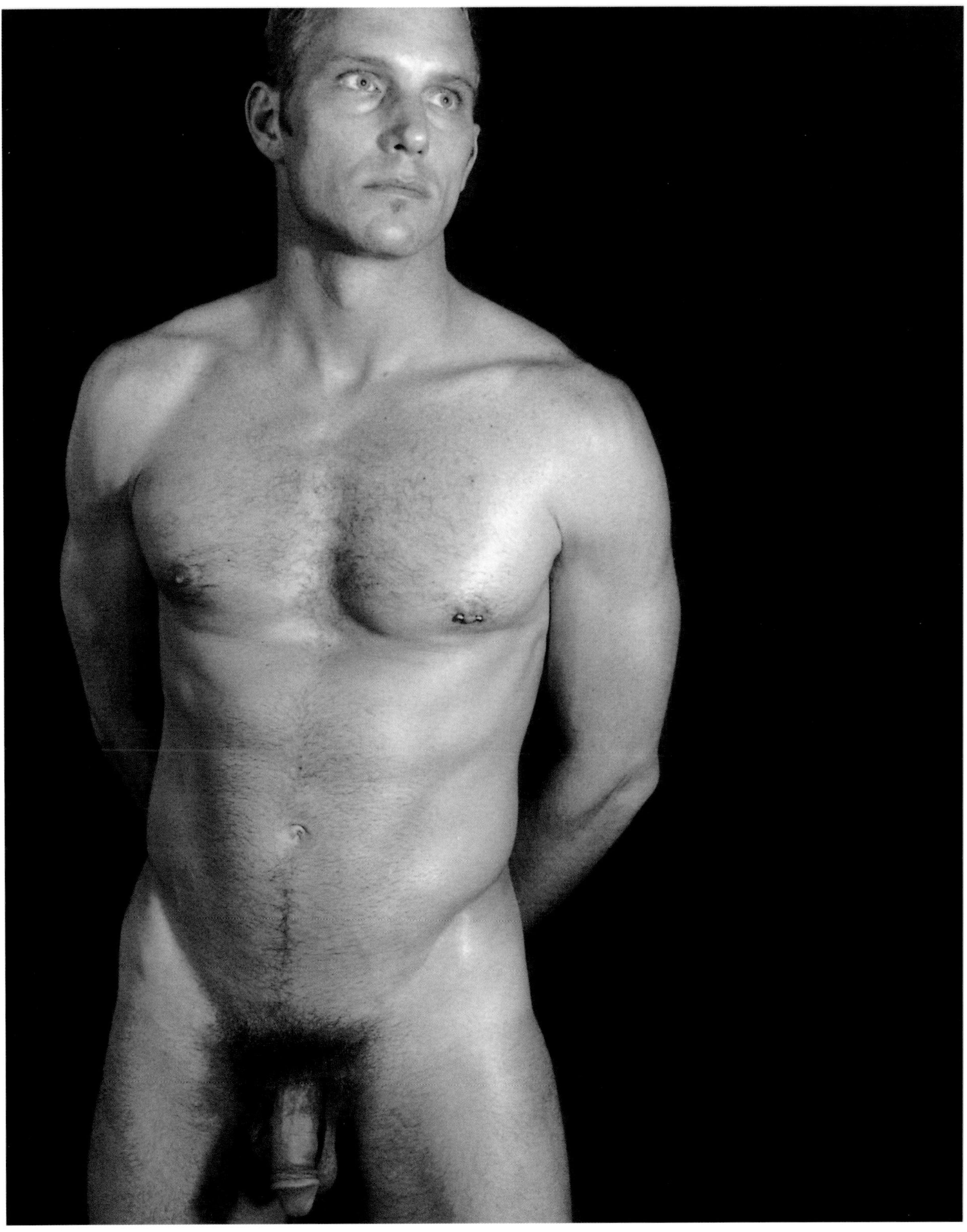

Byron in my hallway, Brookline, November, 1998

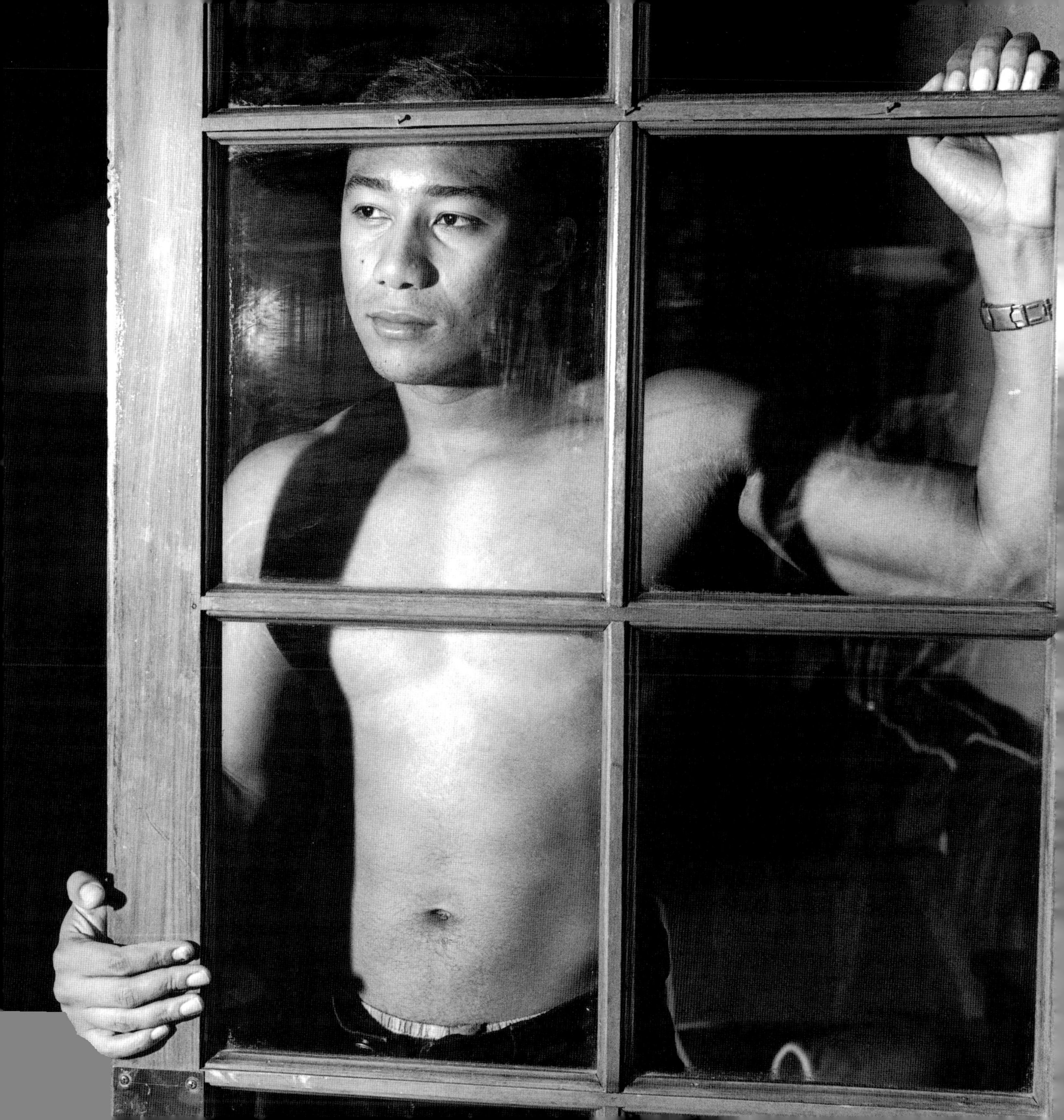

Brian in my studio, Brookline, February 1998

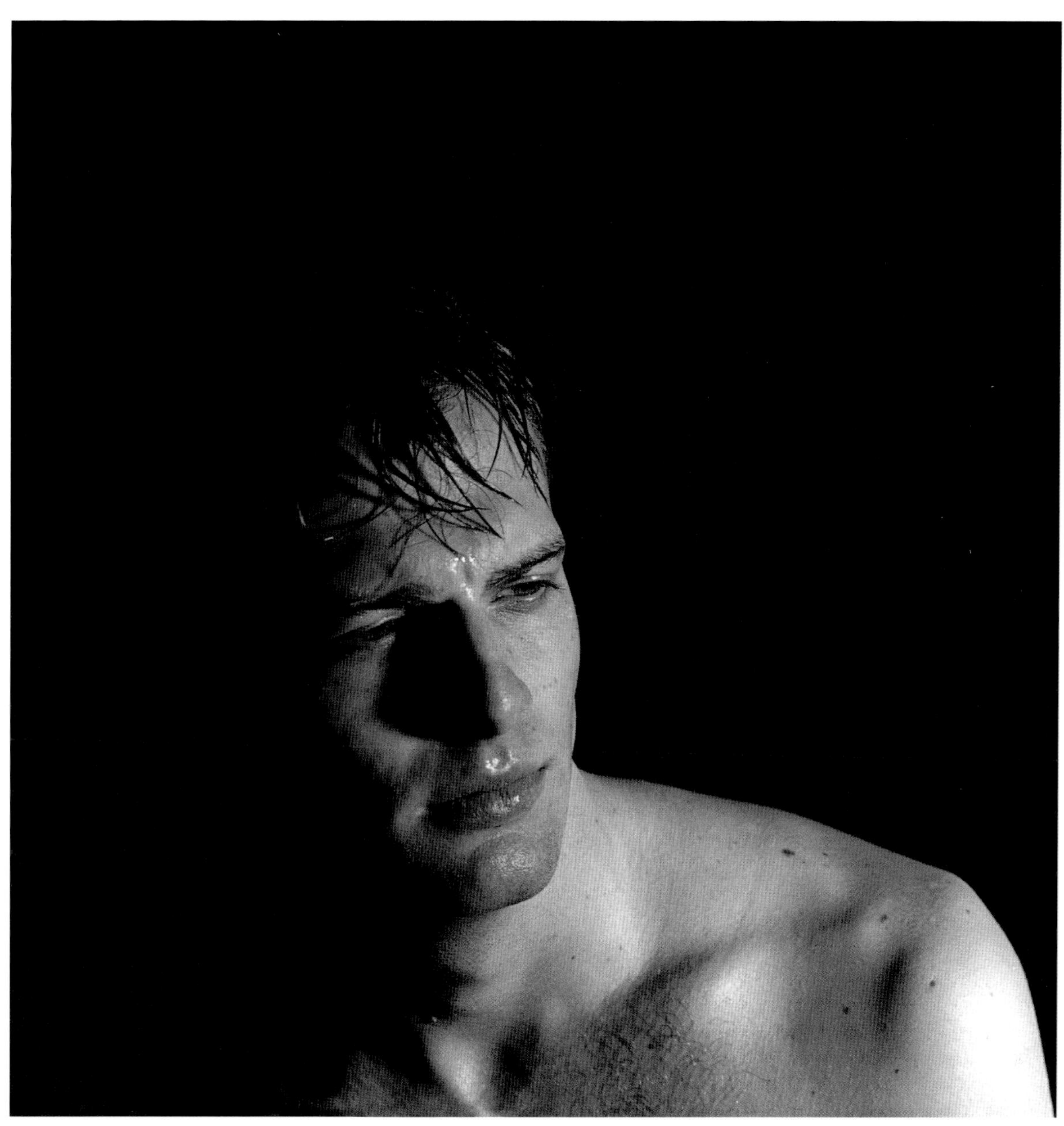

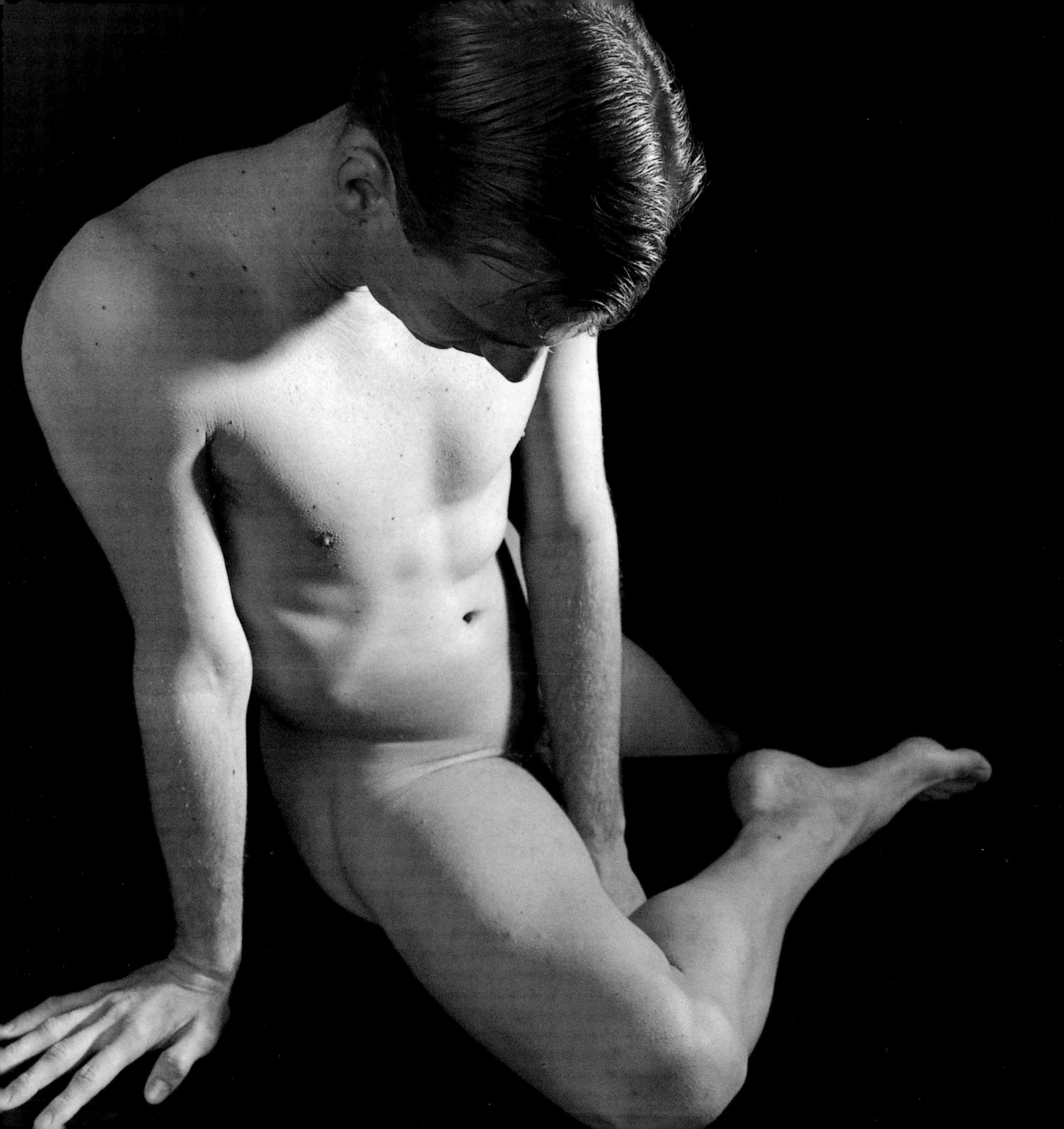

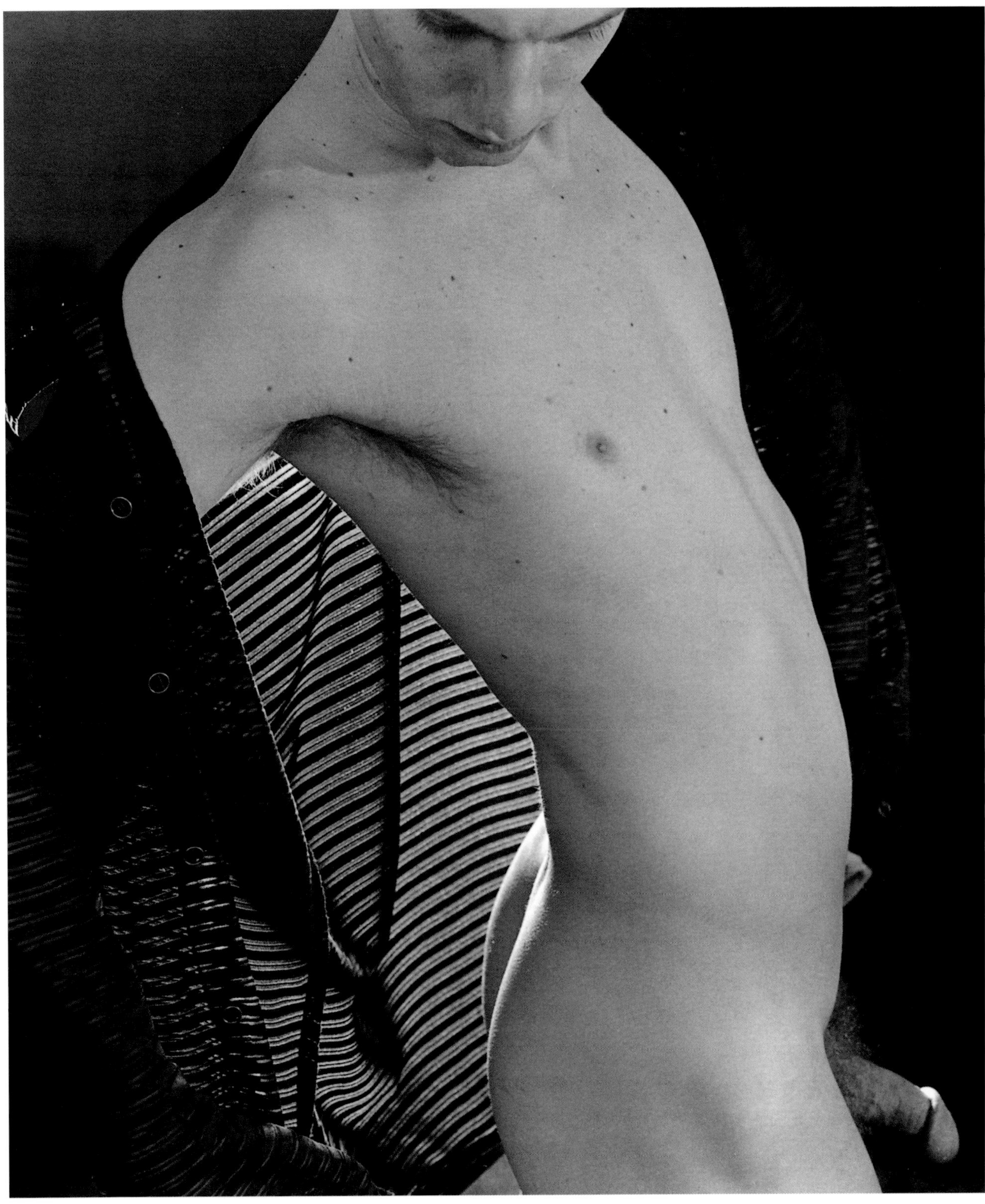

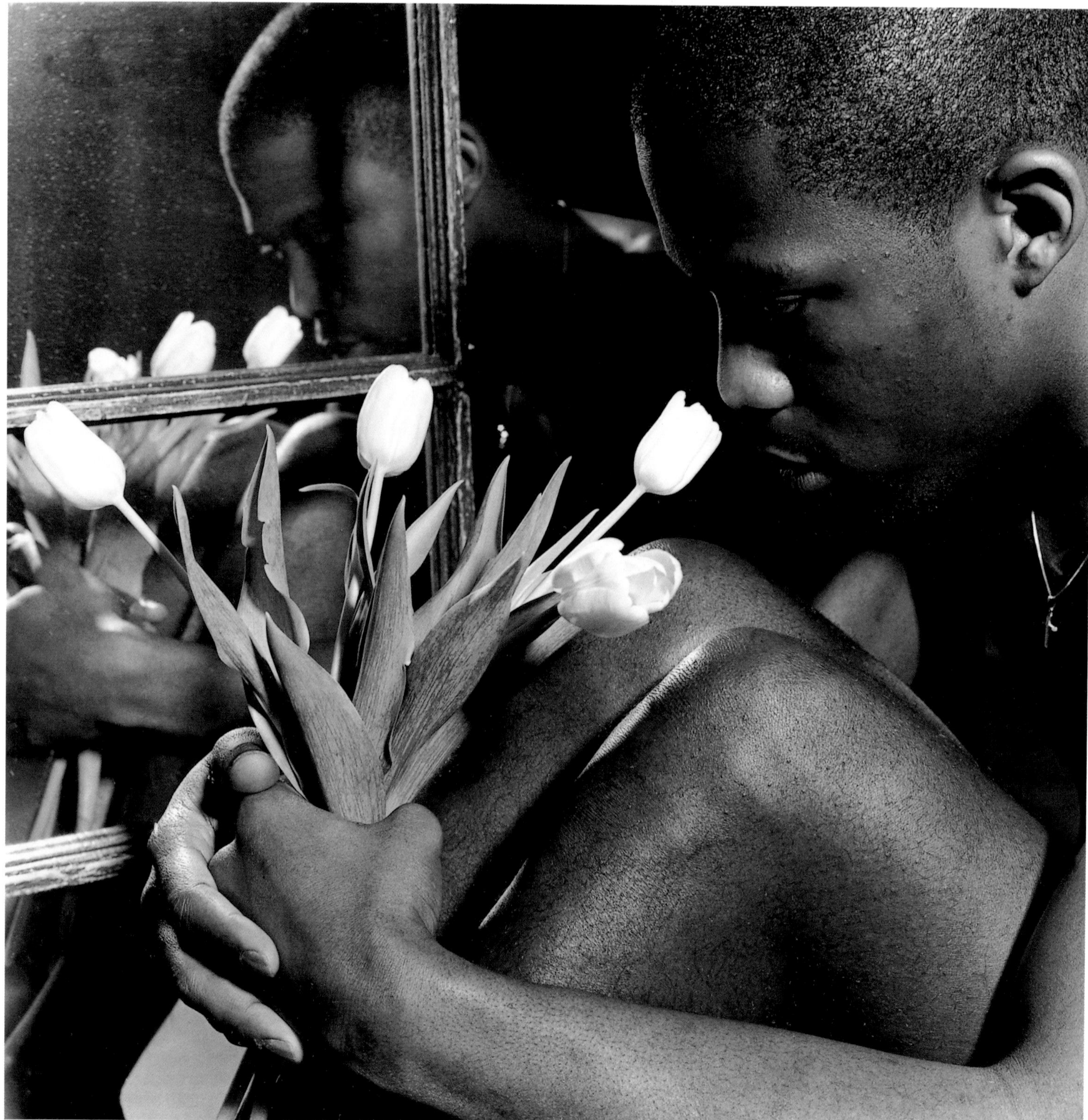

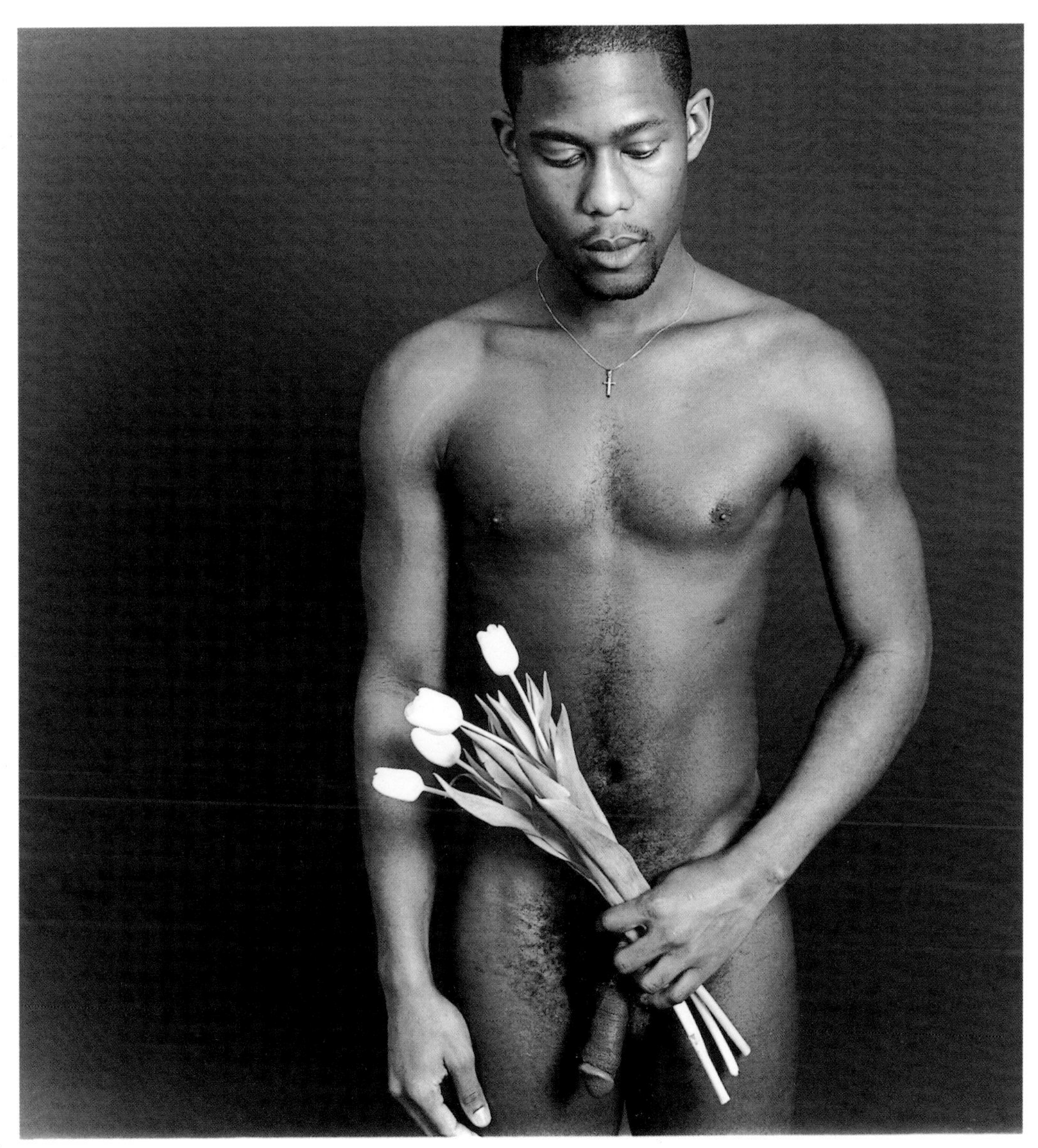

Terry in my studio, Brookline, April 1998

Adam in my studio, Brookline, April 1998

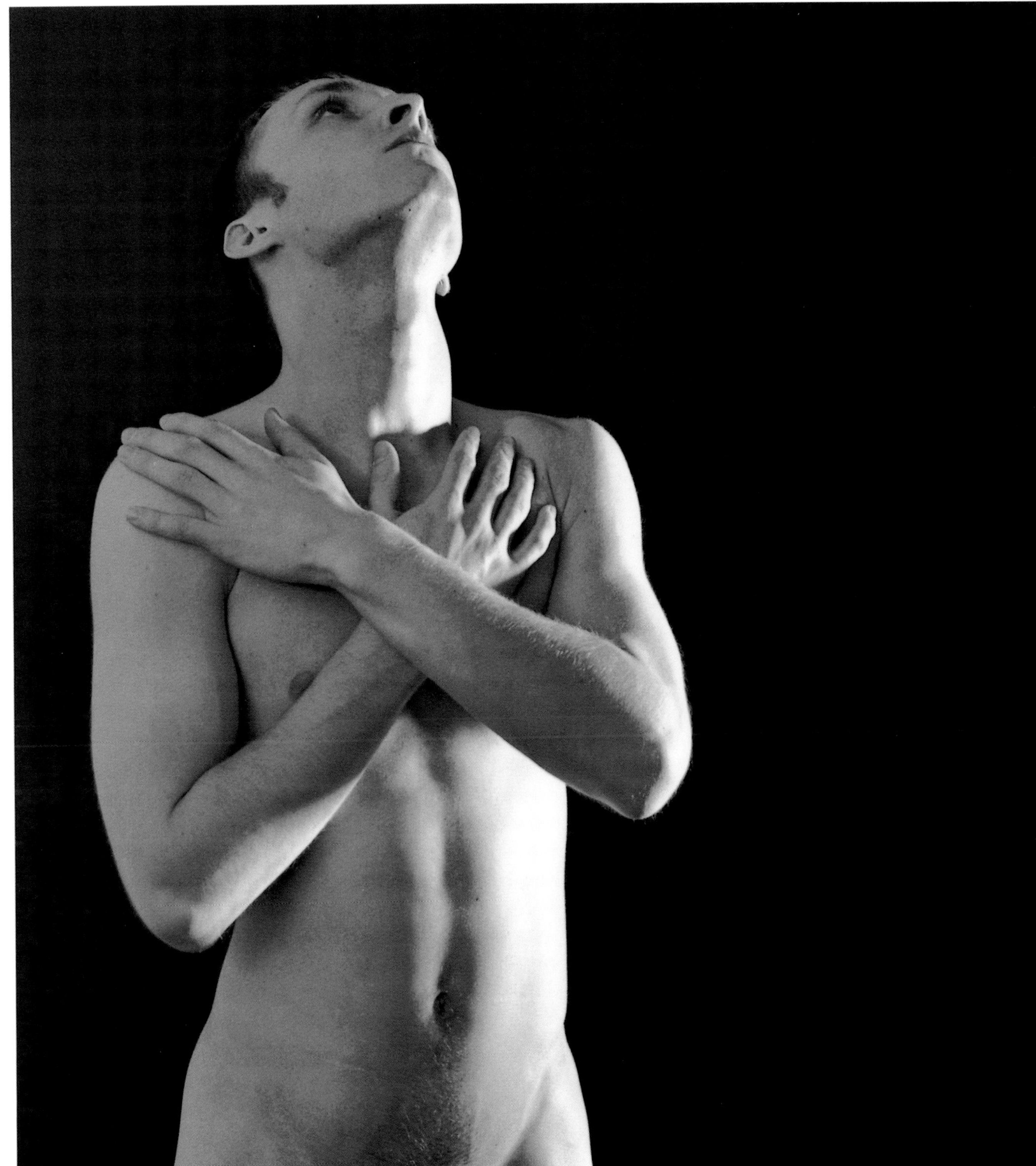

Shane in Jonathan O'Leary's studio, Boston, December 1999

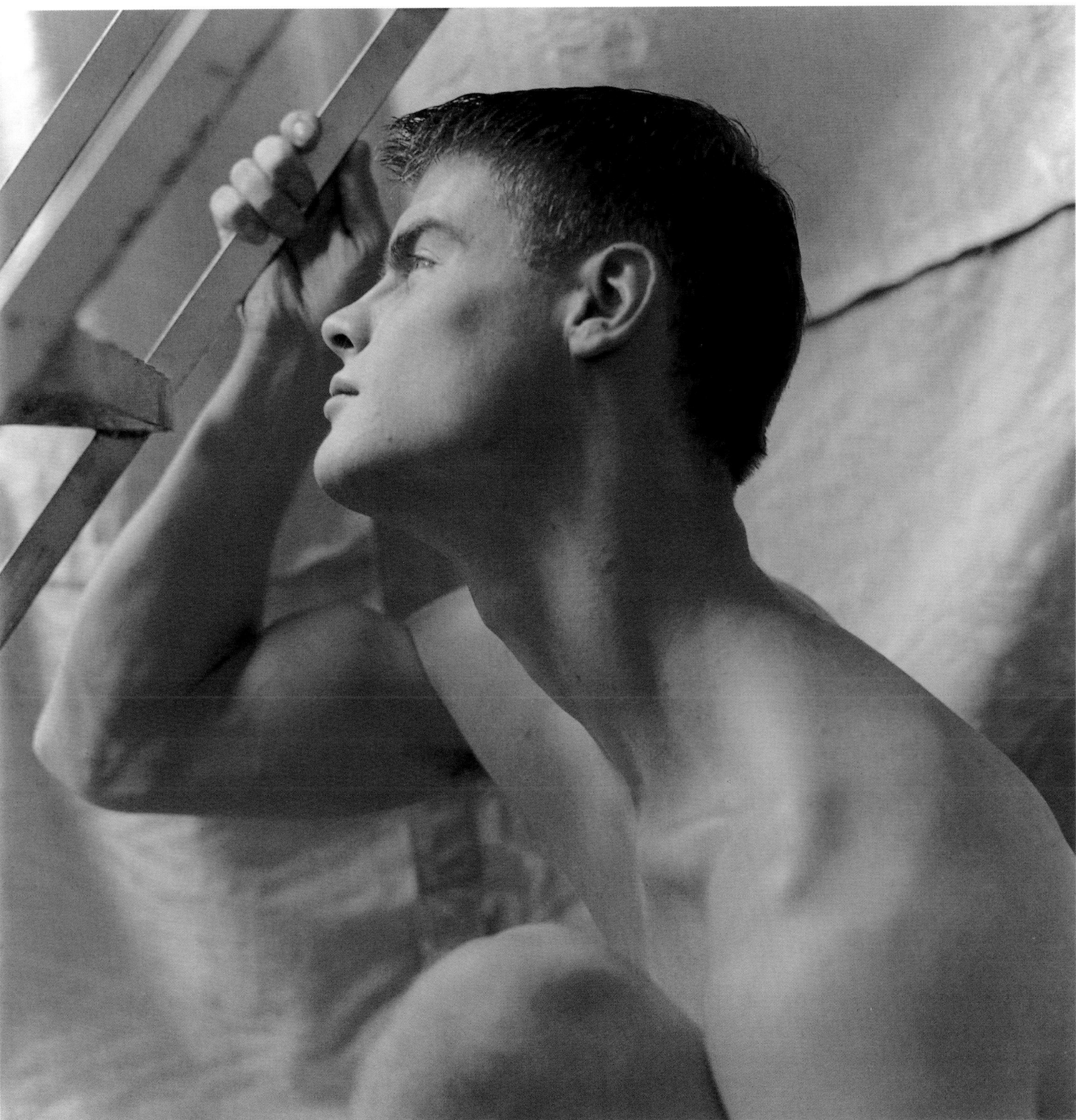

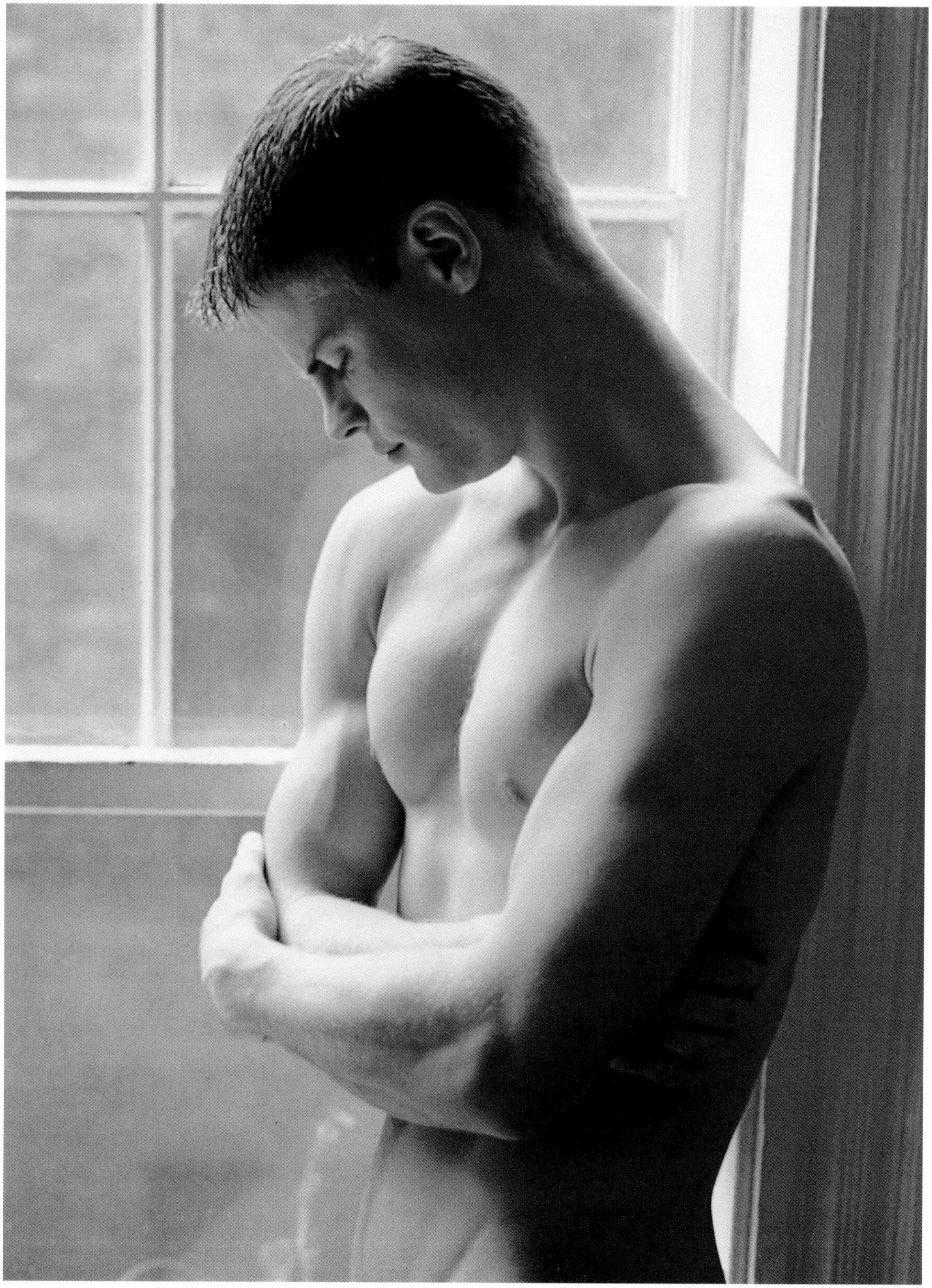

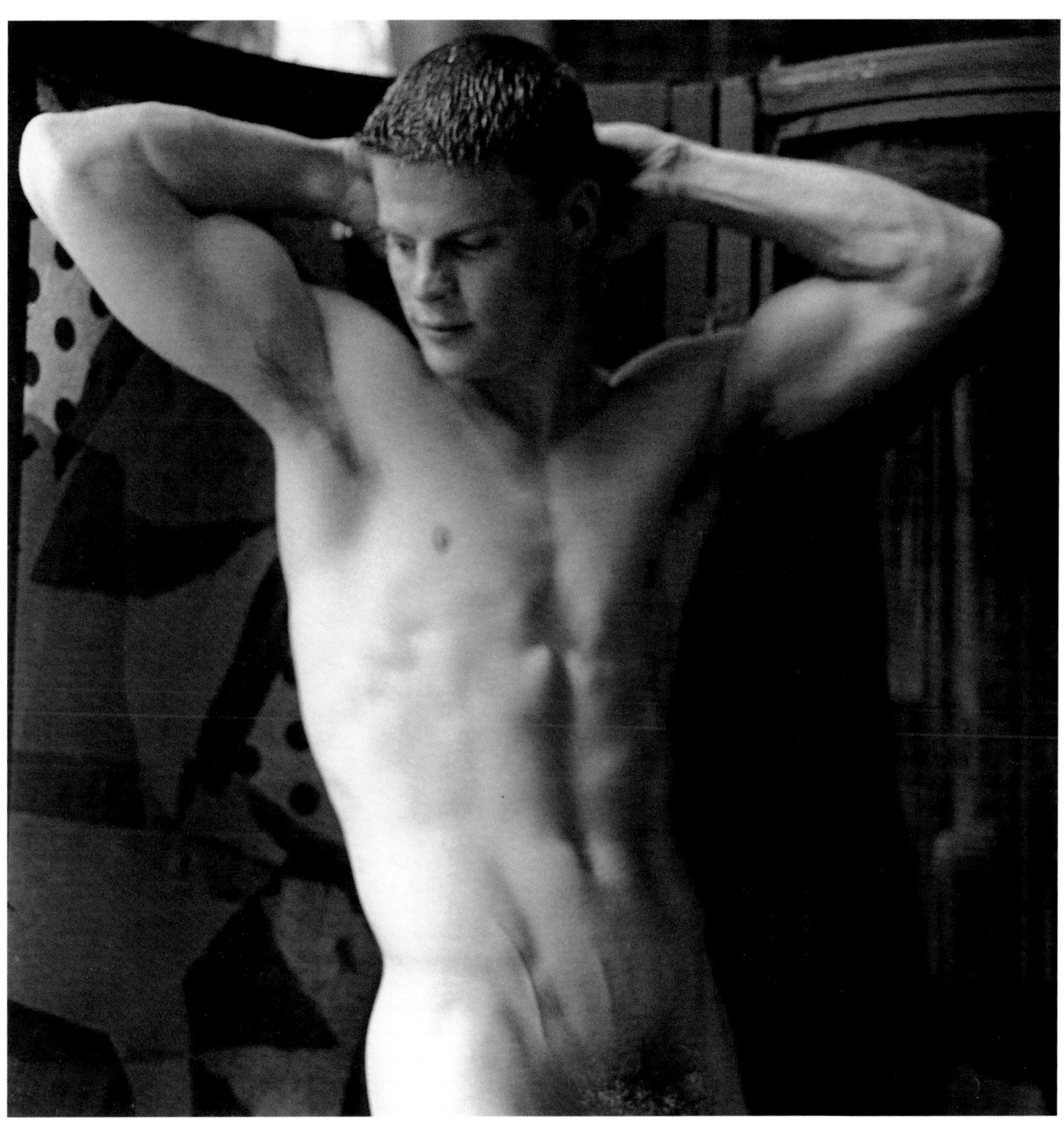

Ricardo in my studio, Brookline, July 1998

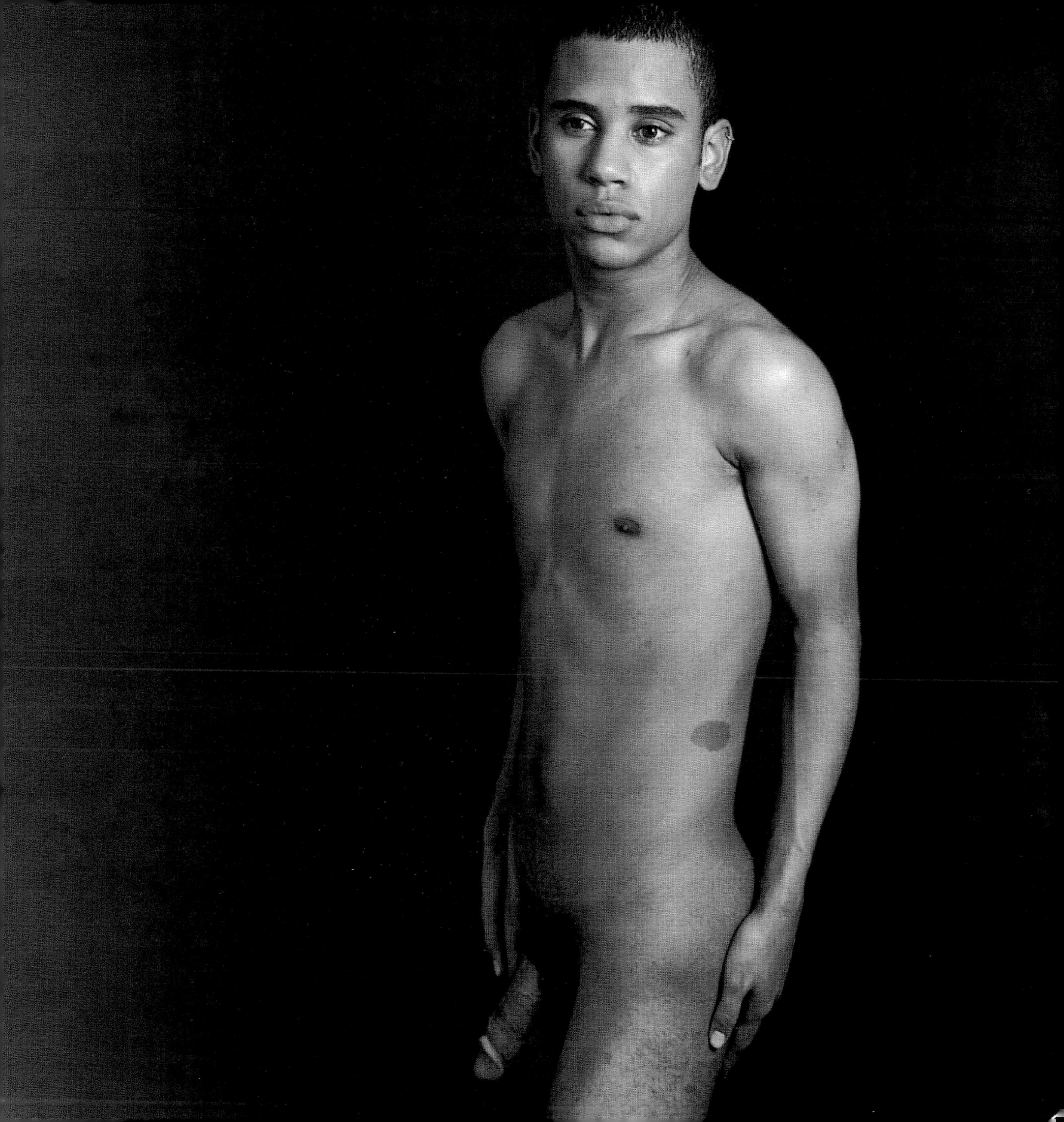

Keith in my studio, Brookline, October 1998

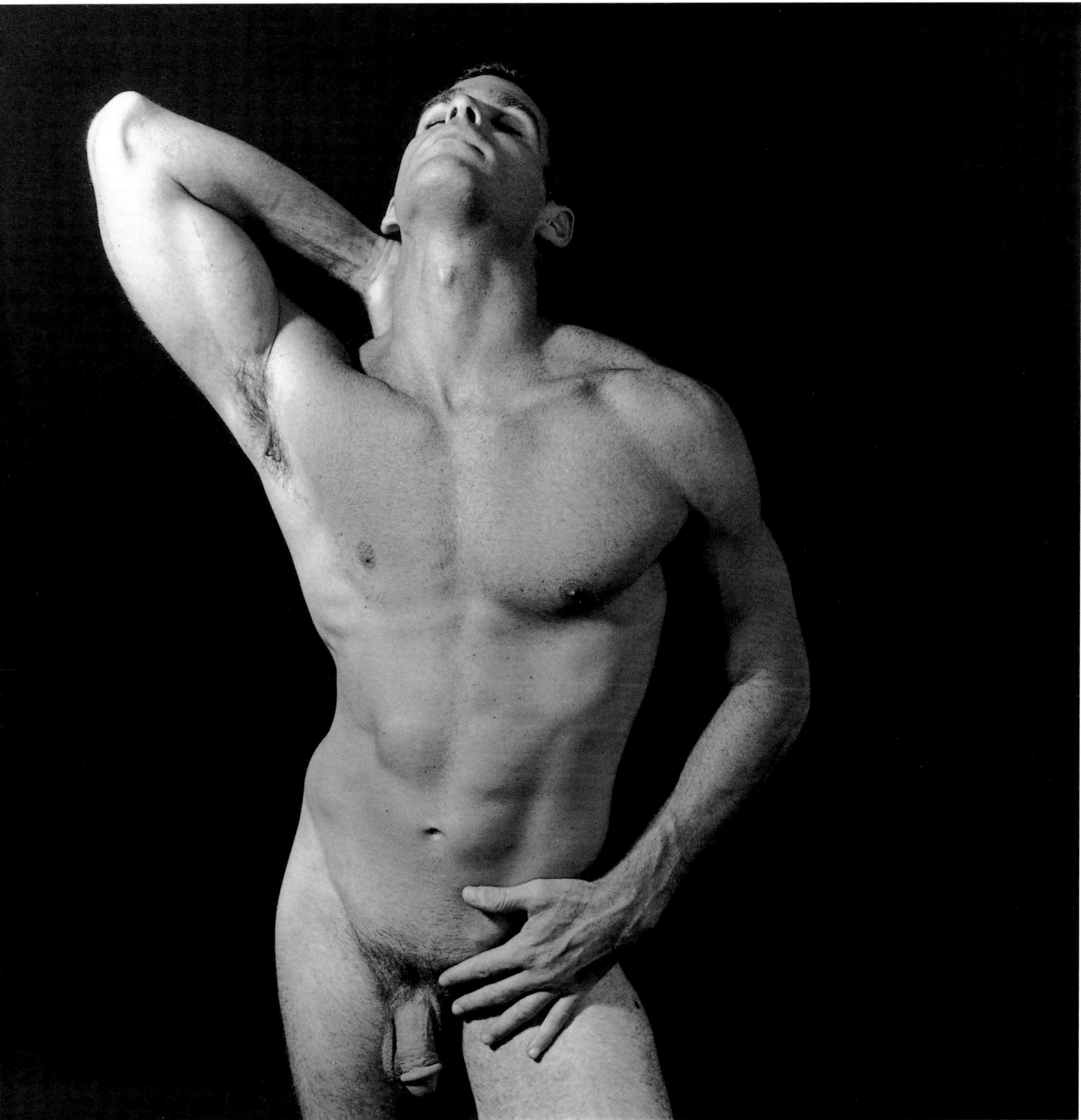

Damian in my studio, Brookline, March 1998

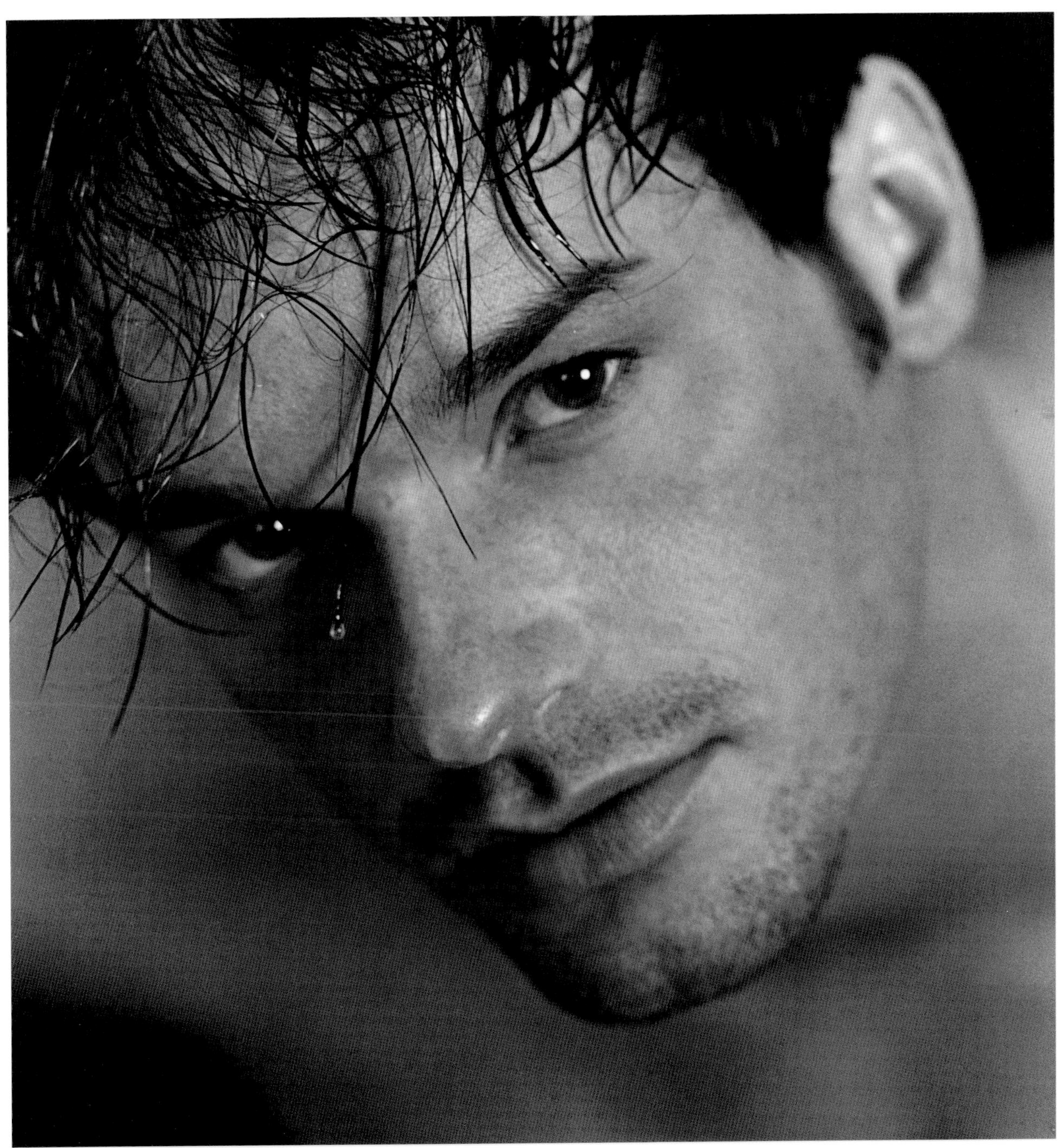

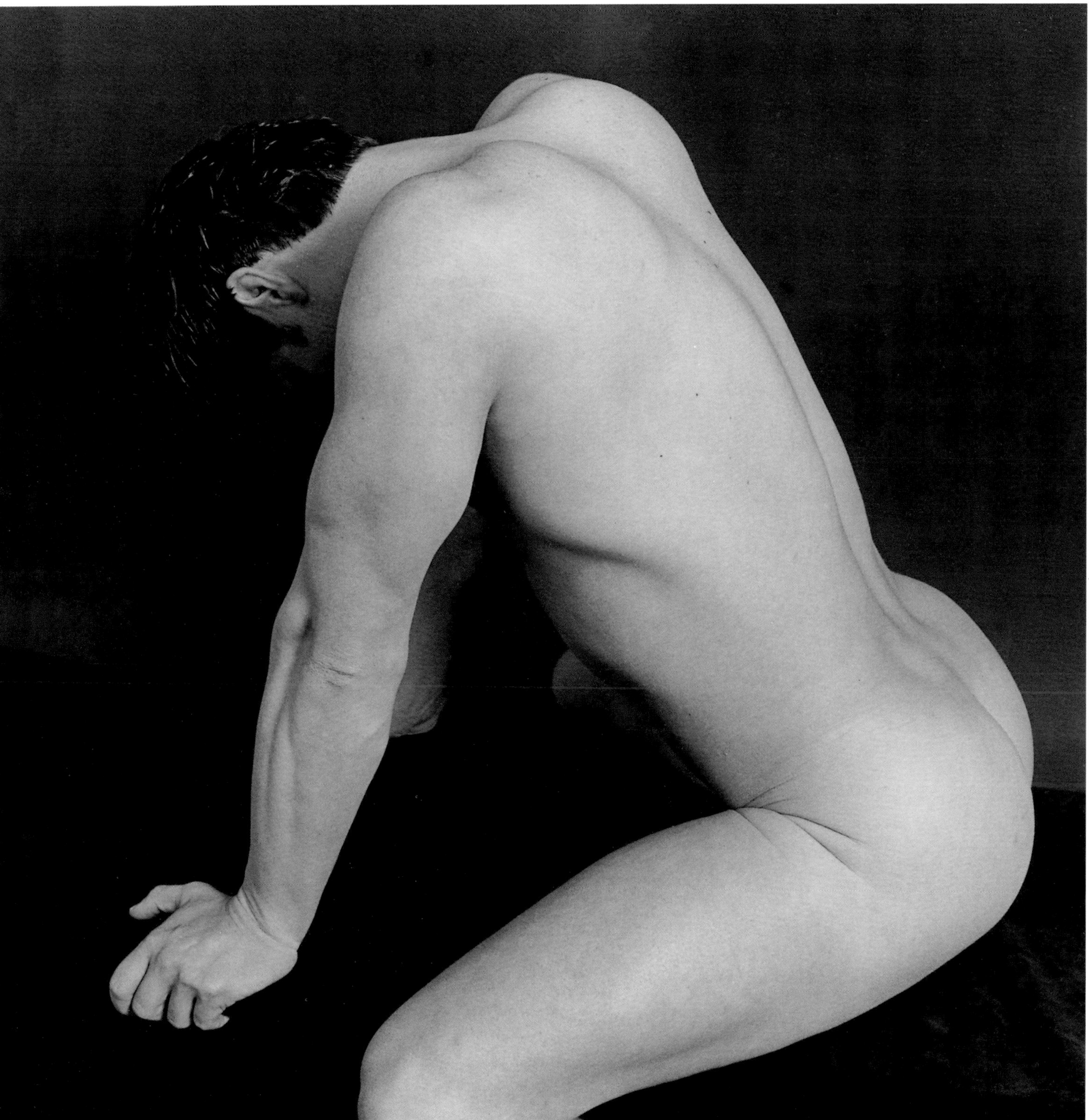

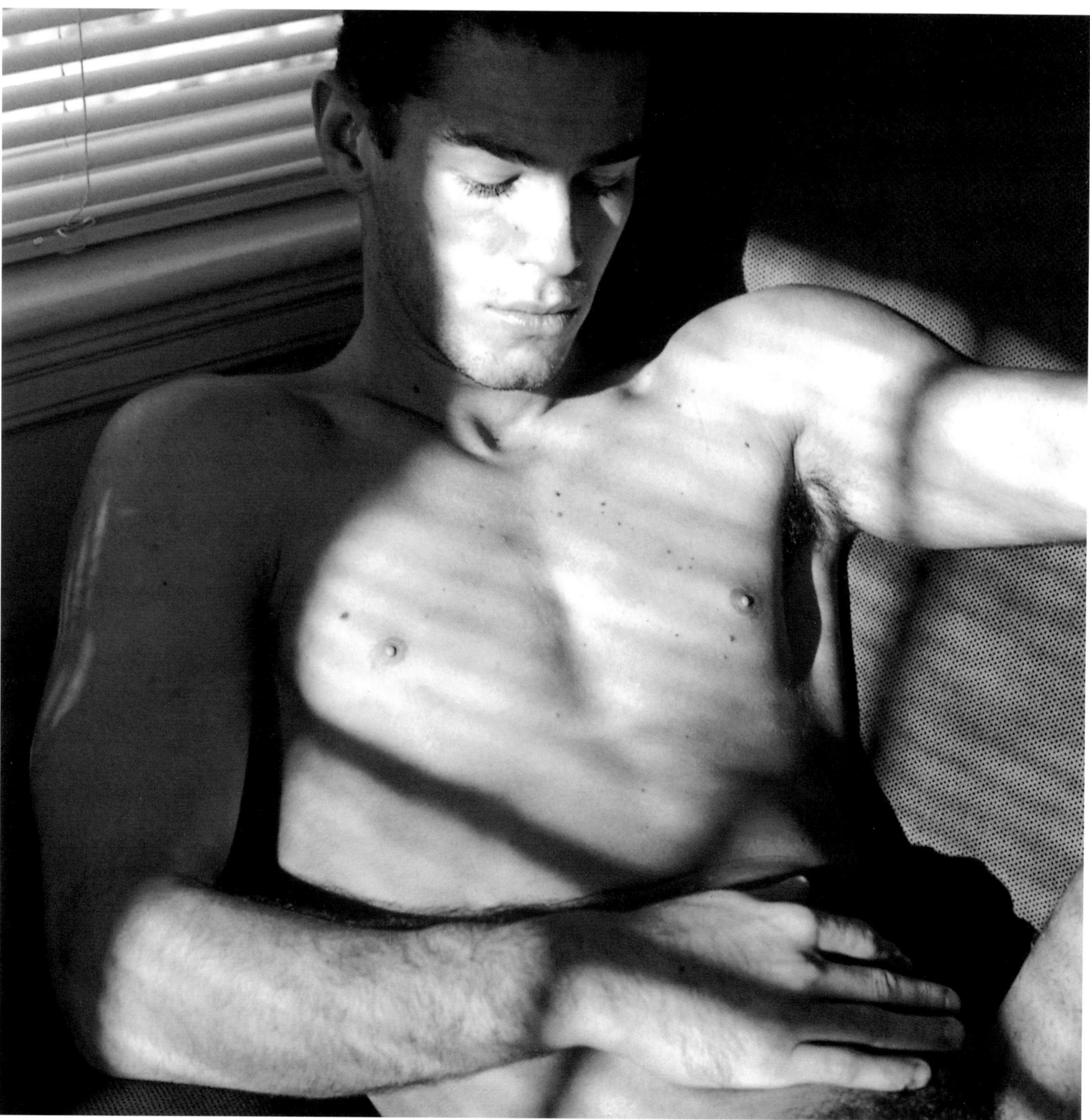

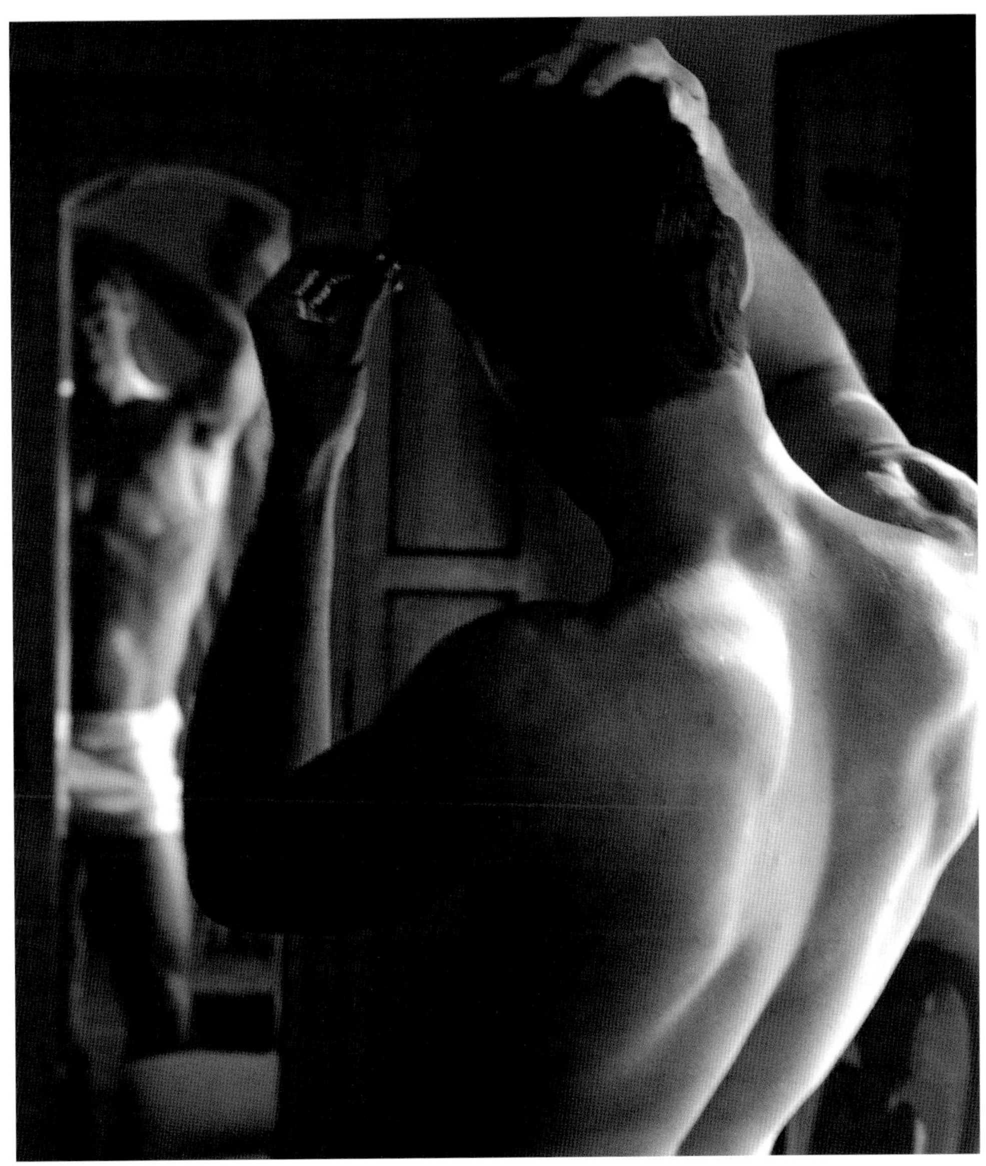

Wanderson in my den, Brookline, November 1998

Wanderson in my stairwell, Brookline, November 1998

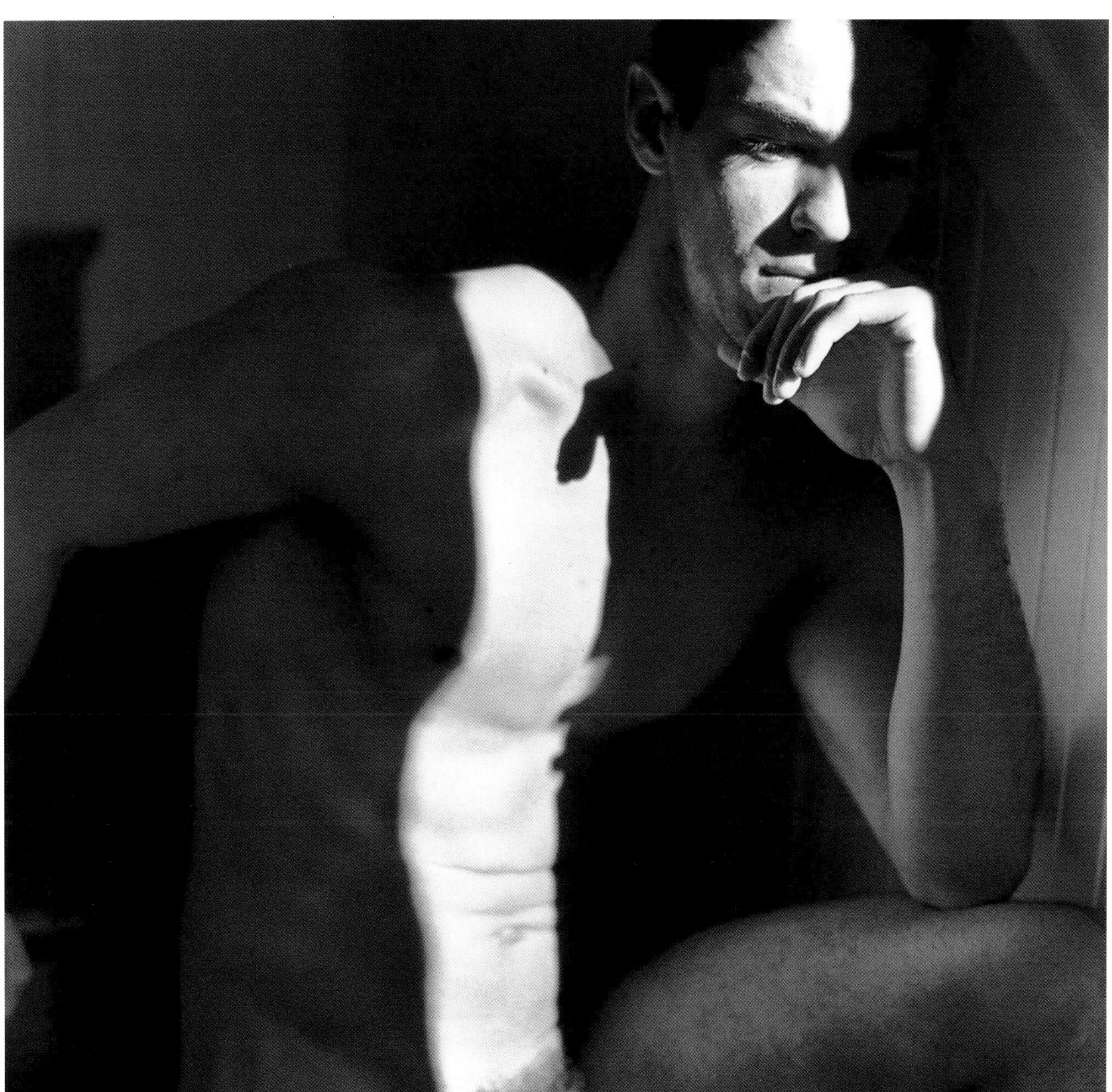

Acknowledgments

I owe a very deep debt of gratitude to Nick Johnson, who encouraged me to pursue this project very shortly after I began to study black and white darkroom technique with him at the New England School of Photography. His eye as a photographer, and his enthusiasm and generosity as a teacher, helped turn me into a real photographer and always heightened my own enthusiasm, especially on those occasions when frustration caused it to wane.

For all their help, advice, and good wishes, I'd also like to thank my partner Terry Brown, Kelly Johnson, Jim Triquet, Tom Petit, Christina Hajosy, Michael Denneny, Karen Gillis, Joe Braff, Simone Rene, Howard Musk, Tim Barry, Francine D'Olimpio, Andre Vernette, Todd Shuster, Christopher Mossey, David Chick, Rudy Kikel, Shawn Hill, John Ruggieri, Laura Van Wormer, Brian Balthazar, Richard Branson, Ned Keefe, Michael Koegel, Don Yelenosky, Glen Sookiazian, and Chris Nickens.

Finally, my deepest thanks to the men pictured in this book, without whom, of course, it would not have been possible. Each one of them is beautiful inside and out, and knowing them has enriched my life.

About The Photographer

James Spada has achieved world-wide renown as the author of sixteen books, including best-selling biographies of Barbra Streisand, Bette Davis, Peter Lawford, and Princess Grace of Monaco. He has also compiled "Life in Pictures" histories of Ronald Reagan, Jacqueline Kennedy Onassis, Marilyn Monroe, Katharine Hepburn, and Jane Fonda.

As a photographer, he has had three one-man exhibitions in the past two years, most recently at the prestigious Gallery One of the New England School of Photography.

For information on how to purchase gallery-quality prints of the photographs in this book, and/or how to become a model for James Spada, visit his "Black & White Men" website at

www.spadaphoto.com

For information about James Spada's other books, log on to:

www.jamesspada.com